D0913824

LAS VEGAS
Insider's
Guide

Save Money, Keep Safe, Operate and Survive in Sin City

Titus Nelson

Henderson, Nevada

Las Vegas Insider's Guide
Save Money, Keep Safe, Operate and Survive in Sin City
By Titus Nelson

Published by: Silverview Publishing
P.O. Box 778268
Henderson, NV 89077-8268

Telephone: (702) 533-4363
Fax: (702) 534-3989
Website: www.SilverviewPublishing.com
E-mail: info@silverviewpublishing.com

ISBN (Print version): 978-0-9840266-1-6
    (ePUB version): 978-0-9840266-2-3
    (ePDF version): 978-0-9840266-3-0

Library of Congress Control Number: 2014909820
First Edition. Printed in the United States of America
10 9 8 7 6 5 4 3 2 1

Editor: Justin Spizman
Cover Photo: Titus Nelson
Page Design: One-On-One Book Production, West Hills, California

DISCLAIMER

The information contained in this book is meant to educate the reader, and is in no way intended to provide financial, legal, or any other services for individuals or groups. We encourage readers to seek advice from competent professionals for personal actions, financial situations, and legal needs.

This information is published under the First Amendment of the Constitution of the United States, which guarantees the right to discuss openly and freely all matters of public concern and to express viewpoints, no matter how controversial or unaccepted they may be. Any references for additional information that we may provide are for the reader's benefit only and are not affiliated with Silverview Publishing in any way, unless otherwise stated. All information is believed to be correct, but its accuracy cannot be guaranteed. The owner, publisher, and editor are not responsible for errors and omissions.

TABLE OF CONTENTS

FOREWORD

Once in a long while, a person comes along who is not afraid to travel the road not taken, to knock on doors, and to question life's players, movers, and shakers. Titus Nelson is that man. He has a remarkable talent for looking into issues and areas that most would find either intimidating or embarrassing. His ability to question and probe our cultural mores has taken him into the mysterious side of life in Las Vegas. He has discovered that the city is a mirror of the darker, subconscious part of our souls; indeed, that which is an essential and unavoidable part of the hidden aspect of human nature that has to be accepted.

Many visitors to Las Vegas have an involuntary desire to experience the exciting, unfiltered ambiance of the darker side of the city, but are afraid to take that journey ... the one that might grant them access to their inner desires. In many ways, looking is part of the exciting process. But having a friend take a first look helps to reduce the often-exaggerated anticipation that most of us experience when venturing into the unknown

We all grew up with the safety of the Disneyland adventure experience, where our senses could be challenged in new ways, without having to hold onto someone's hand. However, the jump to the adult world of Las Vegas is really a quantum leap - for this town has little tolerance for the naive - and a callow approach can quickly lead one to experience the excitement of the legal side of "the city," which would be quite the opposite of one's intentions.

Again, Titus Nelson has been able to provide the reader with guidelines to where the gray zones of the city hide, and where caution is advised. Many readers will appreciate this book for its forthright approach, as it lifts the many veils of the city, and reveals its true face.

He who did not want his name mentioned

PREFACE

Sometimes a book just happens by accident. I had already spent 15 long years of effort to produce a yet to be completed book about the 1971 Cannikin underground nuclear test in Alaska, where 60 miners excavated a cavity large enough to contain a five story building 6,000 feet under Amchitka Island. This cavity was required for testing and containing the effects of the five-megaton Spartan nuclear warhead. I was one of the deep shaft miners hired out of Anchorage, Alaska for that project, and during that mining activity, I worked with a fellow blaster named Gene Hailstone, an American Indian from Northern California. Gene was a former manager, or so he claimed, of the famous Mustang Ranch brothel in Nevada. He also worked at the Nevada Nuclear Test Site, 90 miles north of Las Vegas. His stories about the Mustang Ranch ladies were incredible. His bullet wounds added to the drama.

While living in Las Vegas and writing about Gene's stories, it was an easy decision to visit Sheri's Ranch to interview one of the ladies for background information on brothels. It was that visit (as well as periodically dealing with the question from out of town friends, "Where can I get laid?"), that raised the inevitable question about whether "What Happens In Las Vegas, Stays in Las Vegas." It was an easy, but sometimes scary, effort to do the research; however, part of the motivation (being newly retired in Las Vegas) was the desire to learn about what was happening in the city, which necessitated getting out to see what was going on. The fun part was asking questions and listening to the often-profound responses. The Internet was an awesome resource for this project, yet at times unnerving. Some of the hyperlinks were shocking. Tens of thousands of internet URL's were narrowed down to the 650 that I feel are the most useful in planning a trip to Las Vegas, or that provide information that may disturb the reader as much as they disturbed me, but ones that I consider essential in gaining an understanding about what goes on in Las Vegas. Click at your own risk. One bit of solace might be that I went there before you.

The saddest part of researching this book was learning about sex trafficking. When under aged girls are arrested multiple times, it is a sign that a deeply ambivalent, uncaring side of our society has allowed such illegal businesses to continue. A first time arrest should trigger the removal of these girls from the streets to a place where they can regain their dignity, gain a practical trade, and become productive members of society. This is not a jail issue but a rehab issue. Laws that are putting pimps in jail for life were a milestone, but took too long to pass, and the slow law making process only allows the bad guys to stay ahead of them. I hope the numbers in this book shed a bit of light on the magnitude of this problem.

The dollars involved in the drug and sex industries have tainted our money system to a point that we are highly dependent on it for the money velocity required to stay out of recessions. All these dollars are laundered somewhere. Pimps, drug dealers, and prostitutes buy cars, rent or buy houses next door, buy groceries, eat in neighborhood restaurants, and sit next to us in commercial airplanes. Their laundered money goes into our neighborhood banks. They buy from Wal-Mart, Safeway, and Albertsons. They buy BMWs, Mercedes, Hondas, and flashy Chevy Corvettes and other exotic cars. Their cash becomes the change we receive in each transaction. We are all one-step away from this tainted money system. I hope this book makes more responsible consumers of those who contribute to the various legal "entertainment industries" in this city and helps convince others to become proactive in solving these social issues.

Writing is a lonely process, not only for a writer, but also for a writer's spouse. My wonderful wife had to deal with thousands of hours of her husband being immersed in a computer, progressing word-by-word, page-by-page until finally, out popped the Las Vegas Insider's Guide. Her unending support was vital to the success of this book.

Many people provided detailed information for this book that cannot be recognized for obvious reasons. To the police officers, the taxi drivers, the bar maids, the waitresses, the dancers, escorts, entertainers, hotel workers, and massage therapists that were interviewed for this book, I owe my deepest thanks. Also, thank you to the high school students that were unafraid to discuss their world of drugs. To the many new friends in the city that recommended places to eat, attractions to visit, and hotels to see, you have my special thanks.

Leonard Ojena, thank you for your almost daily encouragement. Harry Golden, thank you for taking the time to read the manuscript, and for all your great suggestions. Ed Cholakian, thank you for your valuable input. To Bruce Replogle, a squire deserving of a great knight, thank you for dissolving the many literary roadblocks on this dusty road.

HOW TO USE THIS BOOK

For eBook Readers

At the top of each chapter is an internal link, Return to TOC that will return the reader to the Table of Contents. The Table of Contents also has hyperlinks to all chapters and subheadings. This makes for easy navigation back and forth throughout the document.

This is one of the first books written with a large number of web links and therefore, as might be expected, pushes the technological limits in a number of areas especially when linking to the World Wide Web. Links that are in blue are directed external from the book to locations on the World Wide Web. Most of these links indicate the actual web address when a "mouseover" event occurs with the hyperlink. Some web addresses are extremely long and/or may not have worked when first converted to eBook format and therefore a tiny URL or a general link, instead of a specific link was used. If a general link was used, and there are very few, the reader will have to search the target page for the specific information. This may be as simple as scrolling down on the web page.

For Print Book Readers

For the print version of this book, hyperlinks to the World Wide Web are obviously non-functional. Appendix F has been added to the book with TinyURL's for all external hyperlinks. Instead of listing actual hyperlinks, some over 100 characters in length, most have been reduced in length to http://tinyurl.com/ followed by 6 or 7 characters. One only has to remember the last 6 or 7 characters for typing into a browser, as the preceding part is always the same. All TinyURL links are listed under subheadings in the same format as the Table of Contents with the exact wording that is hyperlinked followed by the TinyURL. In some cases, TinyURL's would not work on a few government servers and therefore the entire web address was required.

For Both eBook and Print Book Readers

Go to the following web address: http://www.LasVegasInsiders Guide.net, register with your email address and you will have access to all the current up-to-date, hyperlinks inside the book. Because of the dynamics of the World Wide Web, and businesses going out of business, some web links may cease to work.

Should a hyperlink not work, the website may be temporarily down. This can be determined by entering the URL in the search box at (http://www.websitedown.info/).

INTRODUCTION

Most people will admit that their expectations of Las Vegas are a bit different than those of other cities. The slogan "What Happens in Las Vegas, Stays in Las Vegas" has subtly enhanced the mystique of the city and provides a clue about how Las Vegas has quietly changed from a "Family" to an "Adult" destination. The city offers sexual freedom, omnipresent gambling, cheap alcohol, public smoking, pervasive drugs, lots of good food, places to shoot automatic weapons, gobs of entertainment, and enough adrenaline rushes to last a lifetime.

The expectations about what is happening in Las Vegas relate to many activities that are illegal, or are becoming illegal, in most places in the world. Nude and topless nightclubs, gambling, and the well advertised entertainment options and Cirque shows rate at the top of the list of attractions in the largest city in Nevada; however, there are other activities in Las Vegas that seem to be on the "edge" of the law.

All Las Vegas area businesses are legally licensed and display their licenses in plain view, but they may offer extra activities that are borderline (if not fully) illegal. Instead of "Seeing Las Vegas," one may wonder how to "Do Las Vegas" while avoiding trouble, or at least minimizing the risk of engaging in adult activities while in this amazing and tantalizing city.

As one crosses over the magical State boundary line into Nevada, the laws change. If the laws were uniform in Nevada, life would be easy. However, the laws change from city to city, and from county to county, especially for adult activities. In the greater metropolitan area of Las Vegas, activities that are illegal in the cities of North Las Vegas or Henderson can be legal across the street in Clark County. And what is illegal in Clark County can be legal in Nye County.

To confuse matters, the boundary lines are nearly impossible to determine without a detailed map. Within only a few blocks, one can cross over the boundaries of North Las Vegas, to the

1

City of Las Vegas, to the unincorporated city of Paradise that is located in the jurisdiction of Clark County. If one engages in adult interests that are on the "edge," then one is advised to know in what jurisdiction the activity is located. This book will help to identify those boundaries.

Las Vegas is an incredible adult Disneyland. There are topless and nude nightclubs where hundreds of "The Baddest Females" hang out. There are swingers clubs with wild sex orgies, massage parlors with purported 'Happy Endings" (yes they are real), and all sorts of other fun things to do.

One may see ladies carrying alcoholic beverages on the street, and men smoking "them big-ole honker" cigars nestled between the thumb and index finger, or catch a glimpse of a huge wad of money being pulled out of a pocket that ensures the holder is a man of wealth, even if he is only buying a hotdog on a stick. Ladies are eyeing men and wondering if they are available, and men are checking out the chicks wondering the same thing. If you ladies are looking for a tall Male Russian Hunk to spend an evening with, or if you men want to hold a Blond Russian Knockout in your arms, then this book will help you find what you are looking for.

The atmosphere of Las Vegas is exciting, overwhelming, and intimidating. It's an electrifying adult world inviting exploration and discovery; however, when one comes to his senses he might feel a bit of danger in the air. Women might hold their purse a bit closer and men may move their wallets from the rear pocket to the front and insert a hand to hold it tight. Perhaps ducking into a casino and pushing buttons or pulling arms on one of those slot machines will mask the feeling. Before the tourist knows it, that "Little Cash Grabbing Sucker" has been filled with a couple Bens. "What the Hell?" is the only thought that may come to mind.

One with any sense would have to be pissed off, after knowingly indulging in a game where a wealth transfer was sure to take place on a one-way trip out of the pocket and into the machine. Maybe some food will help ease the pain. A buffet is sighted close by and our friendly pissed off tourist gorges on the endless procession of edibles that were stuffed in to make sure a "money's worth" was attained. The overstuffed body waddling back to the hotel room can be heard muttering, "Damn, what the hell just happened?"

After a short nap, it's time to burn off a little frustration. So, our excited tourist goes down to that gun place to shoot a machine gun. A gorgeous attendant recommends the biggest and baddest gun in their inventory. She can hardly carry the slick looking 50 cal. machine gun just ordered. So as not to disappoint the gun savvy lady with the Glock on her hip, our unsuspecting tourist pulls out a credit card to rent the beast. The sweet lady brings out a big pile of neat looking shiny brass ammunition to go with it. The credit card feels a little heavy, but it is handed over without question.

After a brief instruction, everything is ready and the magic moment arrives! The trigger is pulled and "Ka-Fume!" Really big bullets are discharged out of that beast and blast the living crap out of everything in sight. While our excited tourist's lower lip quivers, the lady explains that there are still 29 more minutes left on the clock. Our tourist fires the gun at will and shiny brass is flying everywhere. A quick look down discloses the legs disappearing into a pile of smoking brass casings that cost $5 each and were shot at 500 rounds a minute.

It doesn't take long for the tourist to come up with an excuse to leave immediately, while keeping cool in front of the sweet, sexy, and devious sales lady as she completes the credit card transaction. In the limousine, the tourist's lower lip starts quivering again and the words finally come together in an intelligible sentence: "What The Hell Just Happened?"

Our surprised tourist gets a flash that perhaps a little personal protection would be in order. The limousine driver is instructed to go by the <u>Bass Pro</u> sporting goods shop next to the Silverton Casino. The ladies might think twice before going down there and buying one of them big-ole "<u>50 cal. Desert Eagles</u>" to hide in their purse. Meanwhile, the guys go searching for one of those impractical pistols married to a 410 shotgun called "<u>The Judge</u>," to shove in their pants. Actually, this is the place to go see, and shoot, some of these fantastic firearms. Here is a <u>video</u> showing what fun shooting a 50 cal. desert eagle is all about. Now watch what an <u>expert</u> can do with that mechanical marvel.

As the night starts to get long, thoughts of sex arise. Should he choose one of those sexy ladies in the hotel bar, or perhaps he is considering one of those wonderful Asian massages where a body shampoo is provided by a beautiful near-naked lady? What about those brothels where prostitutes are legal and you get to have loads of fun with your choice of the ladies? These fantastic thoughts of fun in Las Vegas fill the mind and our tourist starts to go a bit crazy when stimulated by the concept of being able to do stuff out in the middle of the desert with no one watching. But how does one know what to choose?

As the previous story illustrates, it is easy to "get lost" in Las Vegas if you don't do some research before visiting. You will find this book to be educational in many ways. This book will clear up some of the Las Vegas mystique by providing realistic expectations of the opportunities that exist in the city. It will also provide some pointers to make sure the fun you have "Stays in Las Vegas;" and it will give a little insight on how to keep the city from burning a hole in your wallet, so that on the way out of town you won't be wondering, "What The Hell Happened?"

The intent of this book is to help you find what you are looking for, to keep you safe by reducing risk, and to expand your horizons a bit. In Las Vegas, we want you to have fun and to go home happy; then, perhaps, you will come back again.

After browsing this book, and with a little planning, you will be able to come and "Do Las Vegas." You will learn how to realize your dreams, have a ton of fun while staying out of trouble, and return home with something left in your pockets.

1

LAS VEGAS AT A GLANCE

SOME BASIC RULES-OF-THUMB

A long time ago when I first visited Las Vegas, I had an impression that the town was sort of, "evil." Kind of like a big leech that took advantage of unsuspecting people's vices, all the while sucking the money out of their pockets. Back then it appeared that the vices were typically gambling, sexy shows, drinking, smoking, and heaven help us, ladies of sex. The movie star names were pasted on marquees and the stories of mobsters added to the mystique of the city.

Today the city has become much more sophisticated, with <u>15 of the largest 25 hotels in the world</u>, dazzling shows, and unbelievable light displays coupled with an opulence that puts the visitor into an Alice-In-Wonderland like world that is sophisticated beyond the intelligence of many sharp engineers. The dynamic and ever-changing city has only one goal—to entice visitors to unsuspectingly drop as much money as possible while enjoying their monitored stay. Remember, the lights in Vegas are not lit up all fancy because people are winning at the slot machines: The losers keep the lights on in this city.

The desire for a bit of sinister adventure must be dormant in the subconscious mind because it sure comes alive here in Las Vegas. One question (men and women) may want to ask is, "Where can I get laid?" Well for starters, if a woman catches your eye, subtly raises her eyebrow, and lifts the side of her mouth a tad bit in a delicate smile, you are off to the races. What if she is a prostitute? Well, you will soon enough find out. If you didn't negotiate for sex, you hired an escort.

Prostitution is only legal in **some** Nevada counties. Prostitution is illegal in Clark County and is therefore illegal in the whole Las Vegas

Metropolitan Area. What? But you thought? Yes, prostitution is illegal in Las Vegas and Clark County; however, enjoying consensual sex under the cloak of legal businesses is an "**accepted practice**" and is tolerated, even encouraged, under several guises such as: escort services, massage parlors, spas, and outcall services.

If an official is asked about prostitution in Las Vegas, the response would most likely be "We don't have prostitution is Las Vegas," and the arrest records will prove it. The crime maps rarely show prostitution arrests. Look at the <u>Crime Map</u> for the Las Vegas area and the (SC) symbol rarely shows up, and when it does, it most likely will be for indecent exposure. Prostitution essentially does not occur in Las Vegas!

The laws are generally directed toward those offering the services and are clear in various city and county codes. In short, the legal department can make life tough if they want to crack down. However, the laws provide more than enough flexibility so that "What goes on in Las Vegas, Stays in Las Vegas." Because common tourist practices are so widely accepted, lawyers claim to have good success with getting people off the hook. This book will help unravel some of the "**accepted practice**" issues and how they are guised under the gala of legal businesses in Las Vegas.

ASK SIRI

Ask Siri is a fun App to use in Las Vegas. If you ask, "Where is the nearest prostitute?" You will get a listing of the nearest escort agencies. At least Siri believes that an escort in Las Vegas is a prostitute. Remember, however, there are no prostitutes in Las Vegas; there are only entertainers and escorts.

Another question Siri might be asked is, "Where is the nearest massage parlor?" Or, "Where is the nearest escort agency?" Both questions are answered with a number of agencies that would supply the requested services.

A question that might seem impossible to get an answer to, such as, "Where is the nearest drug dealer?" will provide some surprising results on how to find a dealer!

Have fun asking Siri questions and receiving unexpected answers, but remember to be smart about which options you eventually choose.

SMART PHONE APPS

There are a number of very useful phone apps for Las Vegas. These are listed and summarized in Appendix G; many are identified at appropriate places in this book. An excellent web page to find appropriate apps for Las Vegas is AppCrawlr.

WHERE ARE YOU?

In Las Vegas, laws on one side of a street can be stiff enough to get you jail time, yet on the other side of the street you can indulge worry free. It is highly recommended that tourists have an understanding of the general boundaries in the Las Vegas Metropolitan area. An example is walking on the street with an open (alcohol) container. The laws that apply in the city limits may not apply in Clark County.

In addition, there are some higher density crime areas in the Las Vegas Metropolitan Area that one might want to avoid. It is wise to become familiar with the crime areas and not let your guard down just because there are friendly people nearby. Chapter 3 has detailed information on this subject to help unwind the confusing tangle of cities, unincorporated cities, counties, and their boundaries and laws.

THE BIG SUCKING SOUND

The businesses of Las Vegas are run by masterminds at marketing and monitoring, and are constantly changing to meet the needs, wishes, and vices of the tourist. The city plays hardball and it is really, really good at what it does — sucking money out of pockets.

Put this picture in your mind: On your way to Las Vegas, you hear a strange sucking sound that increases in intensity as you get closer to the dazzling lights. That sucking sound is from a special vacuum cleaner that has been mechanically perfected by the best engineers in the world to find and suck in money.

The vacuum is very efficient and has thousands of tentacles, like the snakes on Medusa's head that silently sneak and suck money out of wallets. This is the "Medusa Seductress Money Vacuum" (MSMV). If you keep this image in the back of your mind, you will have a leg-up on efficiently using your money while having a good time in Las Vegas.

As you near Las Vegas it is time to hone your Mental Radar Sensitivities (MRS) to the sucking sound of the MSMV. Take charge of your money and spend it intentionally; in other words, get value for your money. Take charge of it. Do what "you" want to do.

HOTELS

Hotels in Las Vegas are huge, self-contained small cities that provide nonstop entertainment and activities to entice guests to stay in the hotel and not venture outside but for short periods. The hotel goal is to have you, the guest, drop all your disposable cash, and then some (credit), inside the confines of the hotel.

The trade off on where you stay in Las Vegas is related to the activities you have come to enjoy. If you are coming for a convention or a wedding, you may want to stay in the hotel where the conferences or wedding activities are taking place. You may not need anything but transportation to and from the airport if you fly in. However, if you are more flexible because you are driving to Las Vegas or you have rented a car, you can save some money by staying in the outlier hotels such as South Point, or Green Valley Ranch. Or even the Marriott at the Red Rock Casino.

The largest numbers of complaints that visitors have about Las Vegas refer to hotels. Many complaints are associated with being "nickel-and-dimed-to-death" as many items and services that are free in other hotels are provided at extra charges (such as Internet; best to use your own Wi-Fi, connect via telephone, or go to a Starbucks). Some of the outlier hotels offer free Internet, free bottled water, and other amenities for enticement. It pays to shop around and to ask about services you expect to be free up-front before you book a stay.

A few hotel rating websites that rate many of the hotels in the Las Vegas area are <u>Rate Las Vegas</u> and <u>Vegas Today and Tomorrow</u>; these may help in making a decision on where to stay. The outlier hotels like <u>South Point</u> where the cowboys hangout during rodeo finals, the <u>M Resort</u>, <u>Green Valley Ranch</u>, <u>Red Rock Casino Resort and Spa</u> and the <u>Station Casinos</u> are typically not listed. These outliers can offer smaller, less expensive rooms and more affordable food options; some of these casinos offer transportation to the Strip and most offer transportation to <u>McCarran International Airport</u>. An excellent smart phone app for finding low cost rooms in Las Vegas is <u>Vegas.com mobile app</u>.

TEMPORARY EMAIL ADDRESS

Getting what you want in Las Vegas requires a little digging. To eliminate a lot of email pain down the road, mainly a lot of email spam, you might want to consider signing up for a temporary email address that you can discard later. Use the email address to sign up for discounts, preferred cards, or when registering on websites to search for adult services. Almost all of the adult sites require a registration confirmation via an email address; so, use a temporary email address to add another level of security while in Las Vegas. Here are the <u>Top 11 free Email Services</u>.

Consider this the first level of dropping down into the exciting underworld of Las Vegas. Even if you do not intend to indulge in the services offered on these websites, registering and cruising allows one to peek in just to see what is going on in Sin City. This is where life in Las Vegas becomes a bit more interesting, below the surface of the visual stimulus seen while driving down the Strip.

Online sites are intriguing to investigate, and they provide very good adult conversation. What is nice about having a temporary email address is that it provides the ability to converse directly with people that are supplying services via these web pages, and this can be as much fun as pushing a button on a slot machine!

TEMPORARY TELEPHONES

If privacy is an issue, purchasing a prepaid cell phone or buying a phone card can add even greater security. Some services will require a callback number, and you may not want to provide your hotel room number. Prepaid phones can be purchased at Wal-Mart, Target, Walgreens, and CVS stores. Some of these are on the order of $25. Now one can talk directly with people supplying services without having to worry about being traced.

TOURISM AND CONVENTIONS

The Las Vegas Tourism web page provides up to date information about most attractions and activities in Las Vegas. One interesting tab is the convention calendar that lists the conventions in Las Vegas by date, including the number of attendees. Conventions provide up to date information on what is currently going on in various industries. Las Vegas is one of the biggest convention and trade show cities in the country and there is always something going on. Vegas Means Business also has an excellent web page on exploring conventions and trade shows as well as a map explorer to find services near you.

SURVEILLANCE CAMERAS

Surveillance cameras are located in all the hotels and high-density tourist areas and in most businesses. These cameras are in place to protect businesses from thieves and should one decide to procure services illegally, a photo will be available to the police and it will be spread around town like wild fire.

In the case of massage parlors, the lobby cameras determine the amount of time a customer stays in the establishment, the house share of the income, and they provide a record to the police departments if customers decide that they want to cheat the establishment.

An interesting article, What Happens In Vegas, Doesn't Stay in Vegas (Anymore) indicates that new streetlights along the Strip by Intellistreets have the ability to monitor personal conversations via video and audio, which has raised privacy concerns amongst residents of Las Vegas.

Appearance

 The average person that comes to Las Vegas looks like a slob. You may test this hypothesis by taking a few minutes to stroll along the Strip. People that look nice appear to have money, and people with money get good service. Looking nice is always key when dealing with the service and entertainment industry.

 It is highly recommended that Las Vegas visitors dress decently (people that look like a slob, will be treated like a slob). That doesn't mean you should be wearing a suit and tie or an expensive cocktail dress. Just at least try to separate yourself from the <u>sagging crop</u> *because even though it may be cool, it's not going to get you far in Las Vegas. So, clean up a little; the returns will be significant.*

Be Polite and Respectful

 Being polite and respectful is the best single thing a tourist can practice in Las Vegas, especially when dealing with the police. Law enforcement agents deal with so many slobs and idiots that when a polite and respectful person comes along, they tend to lighten up a little. When dealing with the Las Vegas service industry, respect for people's time is encouraged, especially when you ask questions. People that are polite will usually obtain answers to their questions and then some. The words "Thank You" go a very long way. Don't forget to tip generously when the service or private advice is good.

TIPPING

One way to feel good in Las Vegas is to tip. The valet, bellman, concierge, maître d', theater usher, cocktail servers, and bartenders work hard for their wages. Don't confuse the sucking sound of the Medusa Seductress with hard working people. If you get good service, good information, or extra help, then TIP. Pack a roll of ones, fives, tens, and twenties and freely peel them off for the service you receive.

Of all the things you can do in Las Vegas, tipping is the one thing that you will always feel good about. On the other side of the coin, don't accept poor service. Report poor service to management. Here are some good tipping guidelines. Note: Some hotels are including a 15% gratuity fee in bills. Be careful so that you are not double tipping.

DON'T COMPLAIN

The more money dropped in Las Vegas, the more service can be demanded. There are some foreigners that come to Las Vegas with an agenda to complain, and they complain loudly so that everyone around them feels uncomfortable. They will bitch about anything and everything, insisting that they get a discount for the bad food, or the uncomfortable bed, or the sour tasting wine. Anyone demanding discounts by complaining, in short order, will end up on "the list."

Keep in mind that Las Vegas is one of the most monitored cities in the world. If you are identified as a complainer, the word will magically precede you and the service may get worse, or you might be invited to leave. Demand good service, but don't complain to obtain discounts after the fact.

LAS VEGAS TRIVIA

Here is an interesting statistic: The density of Latter Day Saints (Mormons) in Las Vegas exceeds the U.S. national average by about 300%. The density of most all other religions in Las Vegas is less than national averages. Part of this can be attributed to the close proximity of Salt Lake City. Mormons normally don't drink, smoke, or swear. In the days of Howard Hughes, there was an upward trend on hiring Latter Day Saints, since they were reliable employees that were not influenced by vices. This trend still carries over today. So, one may want to consider this before blowing smoke into someone's face, bad-mouthing or swearing, or becoming a drunken nuisance. The establishment may aggressively invite those persons to leave or have them hauled off to jail.

State's Rights is a big deal in the United States. It is the "State's Rights" in Nevada that accounts for the very loose laws relating to guns, alcohol, smoking, sex, and some of the harshest laws on drugs. These are the reasons that most tourists come to Nevada. So, keep in mind that Nevadans may not take kindly to being preached at about guns, prostitution, gambling, alcohol, sex, speed limits, smoking, and anything else that one may want to share their opinion about. Just have fun and don't worry about changing the laws of Nevada. If you want to change things, change it by how you use your money!

GETTING THE MOST DURING YOUR STAY

In Las Vegas, information is your friend—the more the better. Be friendly, be courteous and polite, ask questions, provide generous tips, consolidate information, check ratings and reviews on Trip Advisor and on Yelp, make good decisions, and formulate a plan. And remember—Have Fun!

2

TRAVELING TO AND AROUND LAS VEGAS

DRIVING INTO LAS VEGAS

There are many ways to arrive in Las Vegas. Of the 38,928,708 visitors to Las Vegas in 2011, roughly half arrived by aircraft. McCarran International Airport is one of the finest airports in the world. Flying is very popular, but from neighboring states, many people drive, averaging 87,692 per day.

Amazingly over 7.3 million people are making the round trip between Los Angeles and Las Vegas every year. Average daily traffic volume at the Nevada/California border was 42,399 in 2012. Until the X-Train gets off the ground for charter train rides, driving is the next best way to get to Las Vegas; however, driving has its risks.

In 2010, Interstate Highway 15 was listed as The Deadliest Stretch of Freeway in America. A typical drive from LA is 270 miles and takes four to five hours. This drive can take another two hours on Friday evenings, and similarly when going back on Sunday afternoon. The round trip typically costs around $120 for fuel and food. It is amazing that people will spend 10 hours on Interstate 15, one of the most dangerous highways in the nation, for just short of two days of fun in Las Vegas.

Driving to and from the Sin City is especially dangerous and provides law enforcement with the opportunity to take an additional several hundred dollars of cash intended for Las Vegas.

The following tips will help those driving to stay alive and keep the Medusa Seductress out of their pocket.

INTERSTATE 15

Interstate 15 between Los Angeles and Las Vegas was rated number six on the Top Most Dangerous Roads in America. On this stretch of the Interstate, more than 1,000 people have been killed in past 15 years. That equals 66 a year or over 1 per week. A good friend that drove the highway for several years said that he saw a fatal accident every weekend. Learning from his experience, he developed some rules-of-thumb that "saved his bacon several times." The most important was driving the speed limit. When driving 60 or 70 mph, you can survive a horrendous crash. At 80 mph, you will "eat it." Let the idiots pass, stay to the right, keep back two or three seconds, and enjoy the trip.

The desert roads are HOT during the summer and tires have a higher susceptibility to blowout. While driving during the summer, take notice of all the rubber from blown truck tires on the highway. You don't want to drive over, or be hit by, one of these nasty suckers when they come off a truck, so allow extra space so you can avoid them.

Always remember to Turn Off Your Cell Phone; this is one highway where you can't risk distraction. Take your time and enjoy the scenery. If the highway gets too intense, take the Highway 40 turnoff before Barstow and enjoy the beautiful trip through Kelso. If you are traveling during the day the Kelso Depot Visitor Center in Mojave National Preserve is great for an enjoyable, relaxing lunch at the Beanery situated in an authentic 1925 train station.

Baker regularly sees 110 °F, as does Interstate 15 between Baker and Las Vegas. This area is located just south of Death Valley where the hottest temperature in the United States was recorded at 134 °F. If your car becomes disabled at these temperatures, figure that you will need one to two liters/quarts *per hour* of drinking water for temperatures *above 100 °F*. If you have four people in the car and are stopped for two hours you need one gallon per person, so

you would require four gallons of water. You might be disabled
for two to four hours without help.

INTERESTING SIGHTS

There are three interesting sights along Highway 15 before reaching the Nevada border.

Zzyzx Mineral Springs (now the Desert Studies Center) is a
beautiful, unexpectedly fresh water hole located just to the south
of I-15 about 10 miles west of Baker. The partially paved road is in
excellent condition and worth the short drive along the lakebed.
You may be surprised, as was the author, to be standing a couple
feet away from a beautiful desert fox. If you would like a nice
easygoing 30-minute jaunt to see a wonderful place in the middle
of the desert, Zzyzx is a must-see destination.

Molycorp Mine is a huge open-pit mine located at the top of
Mountain Pass between Baker, CA and Primm, NV at Exit I-15-
CA-281 Bailey Road. The tailings pile, now a mountain itself, can
be seen on the north side of the highway. This is the Molycorp Inc.
"Rare Earth Mine." This rare earth metal mine is considered vital
to the U.S. national interest, is the biggest in the country, and is on
a fast-track expansion effort.

Bright Source – Solar Field can be spotted just before Primm,
NV; three tall towers can be seen surrounded by thousands of
mirrors. These towers are for absorbing solar energy reflected off
the mirrors. This solar project using Bright Source Energy's LPT
Solar Thermal System is a 377-megawatt solar thermal complex. It
is considered the worlds largest. It will supply electricity to PG&E
and Southern California Edison utility companies.

I-15 TICKETS:
CALIFORNIA HIGHWAY PATROL (CHP)

From Mountain Pass and the Molycorp Mine, it is down hill
all the way to the Nevada border. Whiskey Pete's (named after
bootlegger Pete McIntyre) can be seen on the Nevada border in
the tiny border town of Primm.

Be aware that gravity will pull your car faster and faster down this long grade. It is very easy to hit 85 mph here with cars still itching to pass. Take the time to slow down, as the entrance to Nevada is known to be speed-trap city. As that big solar project comes into view on the left, it is easy to be distracted. Sometimes as many as a half-dozen patrol cars are working the on-ramps along this stretch of the highway. A cool smart phone app for checking your speedometer accuracy is Speed Tracker.

There are two or three more traps between Primm and Las Vegas, so it is advised to drive the speed limit for the next 45 minutes into Las Vegas. Several Zero Tolerance zones are located along this stretch of highway as well as Double Fine Work Zones that magically seem to appear around the weekends.

STATES RIGHTS—WONDERS OF THE WORLD

It is incomprehensible to many that when driving from Los Angeles to Las Vegas the laws magically change. Many things that are illegal in California may be legal in the State of Nevada (and vice versa), so be cautious and aware as you approach the state line.

THE "M" RESORT SPA AND CASINO

Upon arrival into Las Vegas, the "M" Hotel can be seen on the right. About this time you may come alive and get excited just as you go under the bridge of NV 146 (St. Rose). Now, one of three things happens here: 1) You come to your senses, look at your speedometer, and slow down. 2) You see flashing red lights in your rear view mirror. 3) You skate by indifferent to what is going on around you.

This location is home to one of the largest, well-orchestrated speed traps that nail hundreds of speeders every year. Sometimes 10 or 12 police cars and motorcycles work this spot. The most probable ticket is for: 1) Failure to lane over when an emergency vehicle is stopped on the side of the road. 2) Speeding. 3) Failure to use your blinker when moving over. 4) Using a cell phone or combination of the above.

Be aware that 15 to 20 mph over the speed limit in Nevada is considered a serious offense. It becomes an even more serious offense if the driver stopped off at Whiskey Pete's in Primm for a drink. Now is not the time to mouth off to the officer about speed traps and other condemning things. The best advice for drivers here is to just be polite, take the ticket, and go on their way. The ticket may cost anywhere from $250 to a $1000 or more. For more advice, see tickets in this chapter.

DRIVING IN AND AROUND LAS VEGAS

Getting to Las Vegas is easy and is most commonly accomplished by air travel (commercial or private) or by highway (private car, rental car, or bus). Once in Las Vegas, local transportation is one of the bigger decisions a tourist must consider.

Getting around the city of Las Vegas is very convenient; it is easy to walk, take a taxi, or schedule a hotel courtesy coach or limousine. Many tourists do not rent cars. It is common for people that drive to Las Vegas to leave their cars at a hotel and opt for other modes of transportation.

You can even rent a Segway for a unique tour of the city! However, there is a break-even point of several cab rides a day that justifies renting a car. Renting a car provides greater flexibility, and privacy. Free parking at all hotels makes renting or driving one's personal vehicle even more convenient.

When flying into Las Vegas, it is very easy to take a taxi or courtesy bus to hotels. Even those who intend on renting a car may decide to go to their hotel first and rent a car later when they are up to traveling around more.

TRANSPORTATION

To take advantage of all the varied activities around Las Vegas, it will be necessary to have transportation—your own car, a rental, or a hired cab or limousine.

TAXI CABS

When going short distances, cabs are one of the best ways to get around. The drivers are adept at getting in and out of places, and know the short cuts to get to the destination faster. However, if you are going to leave the Strip and the general Las Vegas area you may want to rent a car. Fees are on a per-mile basis. If you want the cab to wait, you will pay a wait-time fee.

Most cab drivers know their way around Las Vegas and have tons of information. Don't be afraid to be very specific on what you ask for; a good taxi driver will be a wealth of knowledge. For example, if you want a massage with full service, the driver will take you to a spa. He will call ahead and let them know he is coming. You pay the driver plus a tip. The driver gets a cut on what you spend at the spa. Prior to your leaving, the spa may pay the driver in cash.

Note: Cabs have been known to long haul (take longer routes) in order to get more money from tourists. Signs at McCarran Airport indicate the distances and charges for most cab rides. Use your smart phone to get a distance between your current location and your destination and double check the fair. An excellent app for Las Vegas is Vegas Mate. This app will show the distance between your location and common desired destinations and has a "cab check" button that will show the route and cab fare.

If you take a cab, figure $20 for a one-way trip in the immediate Las Vegas area. Prepare to pay at least $3 a mile including tip. A recent price chart showed $3.30 for the first 1/13 mile and $0.20 for each additional 1/13 mile. So a 5 mile trip will cost you: $3.30 (1st 1/13 mile) plus $2.40 (balance 1st mile) plus $10.40 (4 miles at $2.60) = $16.10.

Figure $50 for a 15-mile trip to the Strip from The M Resort or the Henderson Executive Airport; that's $100 for a round trip. A nice website that will help you figure your taxi fare is Taxi Fare Finder; for example, McCarran International Airport to Caesar's Palace should be $12 to $25 depending on traffic. These fees will change quite often.

LIMOUSINES

Limo services are provided for many of the offsite activities such as gun ranges, strip clubs, and even the brothels in Pahrump 60 miles away. These are usually complementary services providing you select one of their packages. In some cases, the limousines are one way so you will have to pay the return trip or call a cab. It is wise to obtain a complete understanding of what is being provided upfront.

CAR RENTALS

The largest rental car center in Las Vegas is located several miles from the airport. Buses run there on a regular basis. Rental cars can be rented on-line after arrival if one is not needed right away. The hotel will call the rental car company and they will send a pickup van to take you to the closest car rental location, most likely not at the rental car center.

On-line rentals should be obtainable for around $50 a day. Be aware that with a rental car, you will have more flexibility, but you will not have the convenience of asking your cab driver to recommend special services. You will need to be more proactive in researching the locations offering the services you seek.

GAS

Gas prices vary widely in the Las Vegas area. A very handy application for smart phones is Gas Buddy. It is easy to find the lowest prices for gas close to your location. Take note that a few places hide the fact that their low prices are cash only. Credit prices may be $0.10 or $0.20 higher. It is a good idea to make sure the price is credit or cash before starting to fill up.

BUSES

Las Vegas offers excellent bus transportation. A day pass can be purchased at most bus stops for $8, and is good for travel throughout the whole city. Las Vegas offers a few hydrogen-powered buses that are leading the green transportation revolution! They are worth taking a ride on.

Need a limousine, taxicab, or charter bus? The Las Vegas Tourism website includes an extensive <u>listing of transportation firms</u> that will provide many different types of transportation to match a tourist's needs.

MONORAIL

One mode of transportation overlooked in Las Vegas is the <u>Las Vegas Monorail</u> that runs on the east side of the Strip from Tropicana to Sahara. If the convention center is on your agenda and you are staying on the east side of the Strip, then the monorail may be ideal for getting back and forth. The center station is located across the Strip from Caesar's Palace right next to the LINK where the High Roller observation wheel operates. The walk from the Strip to the monorail stations can be excessive and confusing so ask for directions.

WATCH OUT FOR PEDESTRIANS

Las Vegas had 95 pedestrian fatalities in the first six months of 2012. The average is one every-other day. There are a number of reasons for this high rate. The streets are extra wide and it takes a long time to walk across them. Many pedestrians are intoxicated and/or are talking on cell phones, or texting and taking photos while walking. To complicate this, there are many distractions.

To make matters worse, most of the service workers in Las Vegas are dressed in black. When driving they are very difficult to see, even in the crosswalk, until you are on top of them. Thirty-five miles per hour is too fast to see them at night. Homeless people on the streets (especially intoxicated ones) are even worse as they may be jaywalking.

The point here is that you don't want to hit a service worker, homeless person, or an intoxicated tourist. When you drive, make sure you are sober, have your friends be on the look out for pedestrians, and for heaven's sake keep off your cell phone.

TRAFFIC TICKETS

In Las Vegas, there are six traffic offenses that the police departments issue the most citations for:

Fail To Lane Over

This is a new law that requires vehicles to move over one lane when emergency vehicles are on the side of the road. It doesn't matter if it is inside or outside. You must move over one lane, or if you cannot move over you must significantly reduce your speed by at least half. A typical traffic stop for speeding will also yield additional tickets for failure to lane over.

Speeding

This is very easy in Nevada, and especially in Las Vegas, as many tourists are unaware of the speed limits. Couple this with people who might be late to work, gamblers who have lost a pile and don't care, or those driving under the influence, and you have a toxic mess on the roads. Watch your speed!

Cell Phones

Nevada's cell phone law requires you to be hands free while driving, so DON'T pick up your cell phone while driving. Many traffic police ride motorcycles and move in-between cars with ease and it is very easy for them to look into the window and see you fumbling with your cell phone. Cell phone distractions are one of the major reasons for accidents in Las Vegas. It is also against the law for pedestrians to be using cell phones while crossing streets.

Not Using Blinkers

Failure to use your blinker when making a turn is the latest driving violation that is being enforced in Las Vegas. It is always good to show your intentions, but many people that leave a pile of cash in a casino rarely have the patience to be showing anyone consideration. So, keep in mind that you need to revert back to thinking like you are taking your driving test and use your blinker every time you intend to turn the steering wheel. This is something to practice on the way to Las Vegas.

Not Stopping For Pedestrians in Crosswalks

 Wait until the pedestrian makes it all the way across the crosswalk, even if you are in a divided road. You will quickly be stopped if you are found moving forward before the pedestrian reaches the sidewalk.

Tickets In Work Zone

 There are many work zones in Las Vegas and fines are double, so be careful!

Tickets for moving violations in Las Vegas are considered *misdemeanor criminal offenses*. These are serious and it is recommended that they be taken care of as soon as possible. Should one be unfortunate enough receive one of these revenue-enhancing scripts in Nevada there are several choices: 1) Ignore it and potentially go to jail and/or be extradited back to Las Vegas from a neighboring state. 2) Pay the fine via mail (increases insurance) and/or traffic school required. 3) See an attorney, pay a few extra dollars to have the ticket reduced to a parking ticket (not a criminal offense) with no traffic school required; and insurance companies will ignore the ticket. For more information on attorneys, see Appendix F - Attorneys.

3
WHERE ARE YOU?

The Las Vegas Metropolitan Area can be divided into four distinct areas: the City of Las Vegas, the City of North Las Vegas, the City of Henderson, and Clark County. There are a number of unincorporated areas in Clark County located in the greater Las Vegas metropolitan area, all of which fall within the Clark County jurisdiction. Each of these areas have different municipal codes that are relevant to adult activities, so it is important to know in which jurisdiction the activities are located in order to know which laws, ordinances, and codes apply.

USEFUL MAPS

Las Vegas Tourism has an excellent interactive map of Las Vegas that shows details down to street level with hotels and points of interest identified. Additionally, tourists can pick up a Las Vegas folded map provided by Las Vegas Tourism at any brochure stand that also shows excellent details of the Strip.

Also useful is the General Boundaries Map that provides a good picture of where the City of Las Vegas, Paradise, the City of North Las Vegas, Clark County, and the City of Henderson are situated in the greater Las Vegas Metropolitan Area.

Generally, the City of Henderson lies in the South; the unincorporated areas of Clark County in the middle (which includes Paradise, where the Strip and McCarran airport are located); the City of Las Vegas (to the North and West sides of the Strip); and the City of North Las Vegas situated in the North and Northwest.

The City of Las Vegas has a different interactive map of Las Vegas with a zoom capability; it is the first map listed on the

City of Las Vegas maps web page. This interactive map shows the boundaries of the City of Las Vegas. By clicking on the Base Layers and the Administrative Boundaries tabs, the city of Las Vegas and the BLM parcels can also be shown on the map.

These maps are very helpful when researching where a hotel is located, especially on a larger computer screen. When using a smart phone, the Gaia GPS topographic map pinpoints your current location and clearly shows corporate boundaries. Usually addresses will differentiate between Las Vegas and Henderson, however a Las Vegas address could be in Clark County outside of the city's limits. Another excellent smart phone app is Vegas Indoor Maps. This app shows excellent indoor maps of the hotels as well as a map of the Strip.

CARDINAL DIRECTIONS

To familiarize yourself with basic cardinal directions, it is good to know the Stratosphere is at the north end of the Strip, which runs generally north and south. The Luxor Hotel, shaped like a pyramid with a beacon light directed straight up, is located on the south end of the Strip. Major streets such as Charleston, Sahara, Flamingo, Tropicana, Russell, Sunset, and Warm Springs all run east and west and are divided as E or W at Las Vegas Blvd. McCarran International Airport is located on the east side of Las Vegas Blvd. An excellent compass app for smart phones is Heading Compass.

It is important to know your directions and jurisdictions because you want to minimize your time in crime areas and you want to be able to determine if what you are intending to do is legal in the location you are at. For example, what is legal on one side of the street can cost you a hefty fine on the other side of the street. So, persons that might consider engaging in adult activities should know the law and know their location.

Open Alcoholic Containers

 Walking down Fremont Street with an open alcoholic beverage, *can or bottle, is* no longer allowed. *"There's no more glass, no more aluminum and nobody is allowed to open packaged liquor (on the mall) no matter where it*

comes from." If you buy it on the mall, it will be packaged in a separate alcohol package with the receipt attached. This can only be taken back to a hotel room. It cannot be consumed at Fremont Street. The <u>Las Vegas Advisor</u> has some more detailed answers to open container laws in Las Vegas.

The <u>Flamingo Triangle</u> (Rio to Gold Coast to Palms) is in Clark County where different ordinances apply. Walking here with an open container is against the law. According to <u>Wise Laws</u>, open containers are legal on the street in Las Vegas but not in Clark County. A good portion of the Strip is located in Paradise, and is not part of the City of Las Vegas and therefore falls under Clark County ordinances. The boundary line is usually the center of a street.

Massage Parlors

You may want to visit a massage parlor on Paradise Road just north of Sahara. This area is located just inside the City of Las Vegas and is in the <u>89104</u> zip code area. This is the "Nasty Area," see Chapter 4 Crime in Las Vegas, and is under the jurisdiction of the municipal codes of the City of Las Vegas. These laws are different from those that apply in Clark County.

Spas

Say that you read a review on <u>Rub Maps</u> indicating that you can get a good massage at the Rio Spa located at 1535 W. Warm Springs Rd near the Sunset Station Casino. Google maps will show the location. It can also be confirmed on the interactive map that it is located in the City of Henderson. Now you know that the municipal codes of the City of Henderson apply to this location. This spa must close at 10 p.m. per city ordinance.

Suppose you ask around a bit and a cab driver tells you that you can get the best body shampoo and massage at Wells Spa on Convention Center Drive. You Google the *name and find it is located at 252 Convention Center Drive, Las Vegas. This spa is not located in the City of Las Vegas, but instead is located in Paradise, in Clark County, and county codes apply. You can tell by looking at the boundary line (located just North of this location) that the spa can operate 24 hours per county ordinance.*

Guns

The City of North Las Vegas interprets gun laws a bit differently than other cities in Clark County, and they are very strict. Where one may be legally right in carrying a concealed firearm with a permit in North Las Vegas, the city will not look kindly on that interpretation of the law and will be happy to make sure that any person caught carrying pays the fines.

It is not suggested that you engage the City of North Las Vegas in a legal shuffle over gun laws unless you have the time, money, and energy, which takes away from the reason you are in Las Vegas in the first place.

An excellent rule of thumb is to know your location when engaging in adult activities. Get to know your location with maps, and use GPS applications that show boundaries. See Appendix A – Maps.

4
CRIME IN LAS VEGAS

The best way to get a feeling for the crime in Las Vegas is to look at the up to date Crime Map produced by crimemapping.com. This map covers approximately a one-week period. If you look closely, there is a higher density of crimes north of Charleston Street along Las Vegas Blvd. With the high unemployment rate in the area, more and more people are becoming desperate and move to crime to survive.

Also, note that the area north of Russell, west of I-15, and north past I-95 is becoming a "war zone." After-dark, life is completely different in these areas. To make sure you don't end up in the wrong part of town, look at the color-coded Crime in Las Vegas map that will give you a feel for crime density by zip code.

Walking between locations on the Strip can be an arduous task especially during hot summer months. Unless trams or the monorail are close, it is more convenient and safer to drive or take a taxi.

The Las Vegas Metro Police Department is a "Don't Mess Around Police Department." The section below on the use of deadly force provides some insight into this distinction. There are many desperate people in Las Vegas and some of these people pack guns illegally and are willing to use them. The police are a bit skittish and assume everyone has a loaded gun.

Las Vegas is a Concealed Carry State; so for those new to the city, beware! Here in Nevada, the police are going to treat you as if you are carrying a loaded gun. It is recommended that you behave accordingly and follow their orders. In general, if stopped by a police officer, be courteous, do exactly as told, and respond to questions with "yes sir" and "no sir." If some explaining is requested, provide it in a non-provocative manner.

DEADLY FORCE EXPOSES
THE HIGH RISK ZIP CODES

A Las Vegas Review Journal article, "Las Vegas Police Rank High In Shootings" says that forty-two percent of all officer-involved shootings happened in just seven of Clark County's 136 ZIP codes: 89101, 89103, 89104, 89108, 89110, 89115 and 89121. Most are lower-income, with high unemployment areas and a high proportion of rental housing. Each had at least 20 police shootings. Click on the links for the zip-code map areas (note: zoom out one click and the zip code area is highlighted or surrounded in pink).

89101 – Charleston Blvd on the south, E. Owens on the north, Main Street on the east, and N. Pecos on the north.

89103 – I-15 on the east, South Rainbow Blvd on the west, Slightly below W. Tropicana Ave on the south, and Spring Mountain Rd on the north.

89104 – 'The Nasty Area." E Sahara Ave on the south, Charleston Blvd on the north, just west of Las Vegas Blvd on the west, and South Nellis Blvd on the east. The Stratosphere is in the SW corner of this zip code.

89108 – Area west of North Las Vegas Airport - Hwy 95 on the west, North Rancho Drive on the west (diagonal), and West Washington on the south.

89110 – Pecos Rd on the west, E. Charleston Blvd on the south, E. Owens Ave on the north, and all the way east to the mountains.

89115 – Sunrise Manor area west of Nellis AFB, N. Pecos Rd on the west, E. Owens Ave on the south, N. Nellis Blvd on the east, where it continues north and west of Nellis AFB.

89121 – South Eastern Ave on the west, S. Nellis Blvd on the east, East Tropicana Ave on the south, and East Sahara on the north.

This compares to a study that was done in 2007 by the Donohue Team titled "Crime in Las Vegas" that shows the highest crime rate occurs in zip code 89109. This area covers "The Strip." It is biased for two reasons: One is the high number of tourists and the "nasty 89104 area" to the north. "The Strip" is actually considered reasonably safe. This means there is a lot of crime in that zip code based on a per capita basis, so when counting tourists it is probably a low crime area.

89109 – The Strip – I-15 on west, Koval Lane on the east, slightly below East Tropicana on the south and north to West Sahara Ave.

SAFETY RULES-OF-THUMB

1. Leave your valuables in the hotel safe.

2. Stick to the Strip in the area south of I-95 and east of I-15.

3. When walking the Strip, stay in a group.

4. Be vigilant and prudent north of Charleston Blvd, especially in areas with numbered streets (1st, 2nd, 3rd, etc. that run north and south). It is preferable to stay out of these areas at night.

5. Be careful when driving or walking west of I-15 and north of Russell, especially at night.

6. Drive or take a cab to the Fremont Street Experience, DO NOT WALK UP THE STRIP north of the Stratosphere to get there. It is a good hike and not the safest way to do it. The monorail does not go to Fremont Street.

FREMONT STREET

Many people want to visit The Fremont Street Experience to see the 1500-foot Viva Vision flashing 12.5 million synchronized LED lights. This is an action packed street with a long overhead video screen, loud music, many bizarrely dressed people, and a number of freelance entertainers. The street is a "trip," but it has its risks.

The Fremont Experience is in the 89101 zip code area that is just north of the 89104 "nasty area." Just drive a few blocks outside this area at night if you want to see what "nasty" means. Fremont Street, located on the north side of the Golden Nugget

Hotel, is where the action is found. There are many monitoring cameras here and many undercover police walking around. Recommendations are to stick to the immediate area, be careful in parking structures especially if alone, and avoid the northern part of the Strip bordering Fremont Street.

If you decide to go there, it is best to be in a group, watch your pockets and purses, and keep an eye on each other. The place can be very crowded. If you drive, lock your valuables in your trunk BEFORE you leave your hotel, or preferably leave them in the hotel safe.

The Fremont Street Scene is getting better and has the attention of city officials. A cover charge may now be in effect and a few new entertainment clubs and businesses are located nearby. Have fun, but be vigilant and prudent.

5
HAVE FUN AND STAY OUT OF TROUBLE

For many tourists, the key to "Doing Las Vegas" is to push the fun part into the "trouble zone" and not get caught; however, the arrest records suggest that many "do get caught" and then pay a heavy price in order to uphold the saying, "Keep in Las Vegas, What Happened in Las Vegas." Because many who come to Las Vegas are naive of the laws, they end up experiencing the unsolicited excitement that the Las Vegas Metro Police Department has to offer. In this chapter, you will learn about some of the laws that pertain to the "trouble zone" activities in Las Vegas.

When people come to Las Vegas they turn into farcically entitled idiots that go crazy while trying to do and see everything within their allowed time limit. Enhanced with a taste for drugs, sex, gambling, alcohol, and everything else imaginable, all are taken to levels beyond what is against the law at home.

A former cocktail waitress described the scene quite accurately saying, "The guys seem to go insane when they get here. They feel that because they are on vacation they can grope, squeeze, and touch any part of your body they want to (by the way this can get you an 'Open and Gross Lewdness' conviction that forces you to register as a sex offender) and they think that vulgar comments, swearing, and acting like jackasses is not only expected, but appreciated, as if we have been on an isolated planet for the last 10 years and needed all this shit."

It is no wonder she quit cocktail waitressing and no wonder "Open and Gross Lewdness" is a common offense for which people have to hire attorneys.

So for the "idiots" that like to imbibe a little alcohol to fondle the cocktail waitresses, just remember in Las Vegas "NO MEANS NO." The "Open and Gross Lewdness" law is there for a reason, and in most cases, inappropriate gestures are probably being recorded.

The service industry of Las Vegas does an excellent job in accommodating the tourist in all areas of interest, advertised or other. This creates an atmosphere of "accepted practice" for many vices. The problem is that it entices many to stretch the law. Be more aware of your surroundings, and ask permission if you are unsure if something is permitted.

In Las Vegas, most people that are skirting the law are sensible, cautious, and generally prudent. They enjoy their drugs, the parties, the great entertainment; they "get laid," enjoy some good adrenaline rushes, and stay out of trouble.

For some people having fun and staying out of trouble is very difficult. For those that cannot resist maximizing entanglement with the law, see Appendix F Attorneys for a list of criminal attorneys in Las Vegas.

Even though this is from 2009, the "10 Surest Ways To Get Arrested In Las Vegas" still applies. Doing a dumb thing like taking a dip in a fountain on the Strip is a sure way to get thrown in jail. Another sure-fire, high tech method is to use a card counting App on a smart phone while playing cards.

Additionally, it is inadvisable to go for the VIP service in a club and then decide to dash for the exit door. By the time you get to your hotel or near the Nevada border, you will get your very own blue light special VIP service complete with escorts carrying guns!

The rest of the ten ways to get arrested in Las Vegas make for a fun read:

1) Drug Related Offenses 2) Drunk Driving/DUI/DUID 3) Possession of Controlled Substance 4) Sexual Assault 5) Trespass 6) Sex Crimes Statutory Sexual Seduction 7) Open and Gross Lewdness 8) Solicitation for Prostitution 9) Pandering 10) Sex worker Prostitution.

COMMON MISDEMEANOR CHARGES IN LAS VEGAS

Generally, misdemeanors in Las Vegas, Nevada are punishable by imprisonment in the county jail for no more than 6 months, or by a fine of not more than $1,000, or by both fine and imprisonment. See Appendix B for the twelve most Common Misdemeanor Charges that tourists are charged with.

ATTORNEYS

One part of the "Medusa Seductress Money Vacuum" (MSMV) is the Nevada attorney. When arrested or ticketed, one will need an attorney to get out of trouble, and while Las Vegas attorneys are good at getting people out of trouble, it will cost a pretty penny.

Your goal should be to maximize your pleasurable adult experience, keep your wallet leakage rate low, avoid tickets, and stay out of jail.

SEX AND POLITICS OF NEVADA

A law was introduced in 1971 to control the spread of legalized prostitution throughout Nevada and into Las Vegas. This law was backed by Howard Hughes, and was designed to help clean up the city, and to prevent brothels from becoming established in the city. The law remains in place today and prostitution is not allowed in counties with a population of over 700,000. See the Nevada Revised Statute that covers Houses Of Prostitution in Appendix B.

Brothels have significantly cleaned up their act since this inception, and are now recognized business establishments in Nevada. However, the law that keeps them out of Las Vegas may remain on the books for the near future. Las Vegas, seeing that sex is a big attraction for tourists, gets around the current laws and keeps potential brothel patrons from escaping the city and going to Pahrump to visit the closest cat houses as best it can, while at the same time using the laws to its advantage.

Prostitution is illegal in Clark County; in fact, **"there is no prostitution in Las Vegas or any other part of Clark County."** Prostitution is legal in other places in Nevada, Chapter 10 – Legal Prostitution - Brothels gives more in-depth information on how one can negotiate for sex and live out sexual fantasies. See Secret Brothels for most of the laws governing brothels.

THE LEGAL CITY

Every business in the Las Vegas and the surrounding metropolitan area is licensed and under the scrutiny of the City, the County, and/or the State. First amendment rights have stood up in the Supreme Court and that is why one will see all sorts of advertisements alluding to sexual experiences. Personal websites for escorts, entertainers, and massage therapists even make mention that the site is under protection of the first amendment. This also applies to the magazines and the personal cards that may be thrust into the hands of unsuspecting tourists on nearly every Strip street corner.

If one calls some of the numbers, there will not be any mention of, or negotiation for, sex; only escort or entertainment fees are discussed. The sex part, which is understood to be "inclusive," is supposedly left to "when consenting adults are in private." The illegal part, (the trouble zone) is kept confidential. If a fee is paid for escort services and then sex is discussed separately without a fee between consenting adults, the line becomes much more cloudy. Of course, tips are always welcome.

For a quick introduction to one aspect of the sexually intimate activities available in Las Vegas, just peek at the Back Page listings. Three clicks and you are in the center of what happens in Las Vegas.

Massage parlors are legal businesses that are licensed in the jurisdiction where they are located. They fall under the rules and guidelines of that jurisdiction. If the establishment advertises massages, then the practitioners are licensed massage therapists. The illegal aspects of the business will take part in private (the trouble zone). See Massage Parlors in Chapter 9 for additional information.

There are many ways to enjoy sex in Sin City. For example, by using a people finder app, one of the smart phone apps in Appendix G, one can find a like-minded person to have sex with. Other ways include cruising the bars and the pool parties, or visiting a swingers club. There are sex movies on the hotel TVs, or if so inclined one can use the internet and indulge in sex conversation with sexy ladies or men that will lure you into private conferences via HD video. One can also visit a massage parlor, hire an escort or an entertainer, or drive outside the county to visit a brothel.

The sex industry is huge in Las Vegas. For an interesting insight into some statistics surrounding this industry, see Appendix D.

In the first 6 months of 2013, there were 2,239 arrests for prostitution in Clark County, which averages just over 12 per day or approximately just over 0.14% of the estimated number of prostitutes in Clark County. This was number 10 on the most frequent charges of the year.

The sex industry in Las Vegas has momentum. Based on the thousands of daily transactions, sex in Las Vegas is generally considered as "accepted practice" even though most of it is illegal when looking at the laws. This can easily be understood when viewing the incredible way the city's network operates.

The consumer needs to tread softly when venturing into this "trouble zone" industry. However, when one asks for something in Las Vegas, it is amazing how fast one will find it. Sections in Chapter 9-Sex deal with each segment of this industry.

SEX TRAFFICKING

There is currently a movement to reclassify pimps as slave traders, to up the penalty to "Life In Prison" for pimping minors under the age of 14, and to deal out 20-year sentences for forcing or coercing adults into prostitution. Assembly Bill–AB67 has been passed and signed by the Governor even though it met with opposition from the American Civil Liberties Union. The bill, as it stands, contains zero-tolerance legislation for pimps who, in the past, frequently received light sentences for gross violations of the current law.

In a recent article in the Las Vegas Review Journal, "Drawing The Line On Sex Trafficking" by Tom Ragan, the problem was adequately summarized:

> *"Silver State residents, political and business leaders are properly outraged by child prostitutes, hookers hassling tourists and locals on the Strip and elsewhere, and abusive, outrageous pimps. They are much less so when it comes to legal brothels in rural counties, women quietly working casino bars and clubs, prostitutes dispatched to hotel rooms, or those working in massage parlors. For the most part if it is out of sight, it is out of mind."*

The article goes on to mention that the Metropolitan Police Department has recently made a grant application to help combat human trafficking. The application indicated:

> *"Las Vegas has become a prime target state for sex trafficking due to the highly sexualized Las Vegas landscape catering to tourists hoping to partake in some of 'Sin City's' lifestyle."*

Specifically,

> *"The grant singled out the city's 30 Gentlemen's Clubs, where pimps/traffickers lure young women from across the country and around the world to be groomed as 'exotic dancers.' These pimps look to 'turn them out' into a life of prostitution after exposing them to ways to sexualize their interaction with men through exotic dance."*

How big are the numbers?

> *"The Metropolitan Police Department's vice unit reported that 2,144 sex trafficking victims under the age of 18 have been "rescued" in Las Vegas since 1994, an average of 126 per year, according to the application."*

"But a police spokesman said the department does not keep statistics on the total number of prostitution arrests each year. 'It's hard to put a number on it,' said Lawrence Hadfield, speaking on behalf of Lt. Karen Hughes, the vice unit commander."

"As one might expect, the multiple-arrest factor clouds the statistics and no one seems to know what the numbers really are. Even the total numbers of prostitution arrests are clouded because "They're recorded as 'detaining a person,' a broad category for many minor offenses cited hundreds, if not thousands of times each month."

Sex Trafficking is a serious issue, and it is important to be informed and aware before making any decisions to participate in sex services.

GAMBLING

The gamblers that come to Las Vegas and win money typically have a plan. Of course, there is the obvious chance of putting a quarter in a machine and winning a tranche of money on the first push of the button. However, to ensure that you do not lose more than you want to, and to ensure some winnings are in your pocket upon departure, it is best to have a plan.

A plan can be as simple as having a gambling limit for each day, as well as a limit for your entire stay in Las Vegas. Chapter 8 Gambling provides at least one easy and foolproof plan that ensures you will not lose the entire amount of money allocated for gambling.

Casino Markers

For those that might consider borrowing money from the Casino to gamble with, here is a warning from the Potter Law Offices:

"Las Vegas is one of the most popular places to visit in the country. When visiting Las Vegas, some individuals make the error of taking a loan from a casino and leaving without paying back the debt. It is not difficult for most individuals to procure a loan, or what's called a 'casino marker.' These common casino loans, because of the ease of which these loans can be obtained, can lead honest individuals into serious legal problems.

Since Nevada is one of the most common places for a casino to exist, the laws which help the casinos recover their debts are much more aggressive in the State of Nevada than in any other state. According to Nevada statutes, getting a casino marker and not repaying the debt is legally similar to writing a bad check in most other states. This can put the individual who received the loan at risk for felony charges; including both civil and criminal penalties."

This all adds up to a person from a neighboring state being eligible for extradition back to Nevada for prosecution.

Minors

In Las Vegas, the legal drinking and gambling age is 21. See Las Vegas Leisure Guide's Frequently Asked Questions web page for a full discussion. A person is no longer a minor when they turn 18 years of age; however, if a person is under 21 they are NOT permitted to gamble or consume alcoholic beverages in Nevada. A youth of 18 can enjoy nightclubs where alcoholic beverages are NOT served. A favorite place for those that have just turned 18 is Little Darlings, a totally nude adult nightclub. See Nude Clubs in Chapter 6.

AGE OF CONSENT

The age of consent in Nevada is 16 years old. For you guys that are getting the shakes, here is a "must read" article: Dude, she can't even get a driver's license. Below is an excerpt from the article:

"In Nevada, statutory rape is legally known as statutory sexual seduction, and is defined as consensual sexual penetration committed by a person 18 years of age or older with a person under the age of 16 years. Sexual penetration means ANY type of penetration; that includes fingering, vaginal intercourse, anal sex, and oral sex. It does not matter if they say, 'yes' to sex; it is still illegal!

Yes! Statutory rape is illegal in Nevada. If the perpetrator is 21 years of age or older, they can be convicted of a felony (yep, that means jail time). If the perpetrator is under the age of 21, they can be sent to jail and/or be charged a $2,000 fine."

For more information, see <u>Nevada Statutory Seduction Law Explained</u> and the Nevada Statute for Statutory Sexual Seduction in Appendix B.

If a young lady reaches out with a temptation, a word from the wise is "be careful." Engaging with a lady under the age of 18 that is dealing in prostitution, besides being illegal, would also carry the charge of contributing to the delinquency of a minor.

Some ladies cannot prove their age; they use illegal IDs and they are very convincing. Therefore, one needs to be very careful. If the seductress is a policewoman or is wired, then the adult can be arrested on the spot. The 'Key Question" one might ask when engaging in conversation with a lady of the night is, "Do you have a card?" This refers to her required Escort Card.

Escorting is one of the only legal means of selling personal, more intimate services in Las Vegas. If the lady's answer is, "No," then this should end the conversation. If the answer is, "Yes," then the next question might be, "Let me see it please?"

One might even take a picture of the Escort Card before negotiating for an escort service. An escort must be at least 21 years old. Be a wise consumer here, and don't support "trafficking" of young ladies.

Here is a short legal discussion on <u>Escort Services</u> and being ripped off.

In case one thinks that the Nevada age of consent is too young, 26 other states recognize the same age or lower. <u>Age of consent</u> is 13 in New Mexico, and 14 in Mississippi, Maine, Iowa, and Hawaii.

GUNS – CONCEALED CARRY

A concealed weapon should not be carried in Nevada unless you are a peace officer with the privilege of carrying a firearm, or you have a Concealed Carry permit from the State of Nevada, or a permit from a recognized state.

For persons that live out-of-state, visit the <u>Nevada Department of Public Safety's</u> out-of-state concealed weapons web page or telephone the office at 775-684-4808 to see if your state CCW permit is recognized.

There are many <u>CCW permits in Nevada</u> for state and out-of-state residents, and the best advice is to assume that everyone carries a weapon. In general when visiting Las Vegas, the Rule-of-Thumb is to leave your firearms home. The CCW laws for the Las Vegas area vary from locality to locality. Some hotels have signs that firearms are not allowed.

The laws are different in Las Vegas, North Las Vegas, Clark County, the City of Henderson, and the City of Boulder, and it is not easy to know your exact location; see Appendix A – Maps and Appendix C – Guns.

General rules apply for not carrying a firearm into post offices or federal buildings, so a car gun safe is recommended. In general, a person that wants to carry in Nevada needs a Nevada CCW permit. Information on application based <u>Non-Resident CCW</u> permits is available at <u>Handgunlaw.us</u>. Also provided at this website are a number of links that cover CCW permits that anyone carrying in Las Vegas should become familiar with.

CCW PERMITS AND HOTELS

A person who is carrying a gun into a hotel should take his permit to the security window and let them know a firearm is being carried. Security will most likely take possession of the firearm and return it upon departing. If anyone notices a person is carrying, or suspects it, security may ask the person if they are carrying and if so, ask them to leave, or to turn their firearm into security.

Should a hotel have a "no guns allowed" sign then the firearm needs to be left in the car. If a person carrying is caught with a concealed weapon, they will be asked to leave the hotel. From then on, trespassing laws would apply and an arrest can be made.

A security officer at a hotel indicated that if they don't see a firearm then they are not bothered by it. However, if a gun is *seen* (not suspected by a bulge under your shirt) then you could be "brandishing a weapon" and that law will apply especially if the hotel has a "No Firearms" sign displayed. Pretending to have a firearm is also against the law.

DRUGS

Most people that are into drugs already know how to obtain them, so how to obtain drugs is not part of this book. However, it may be more important for drug users to know what the laws are so that they can take reasonable precautions to reduce the risks associated with drug use.

Drug abuse is frowned upon in Las Vegas, but like other adult activities, drug use is also nearly an "accepted practice." Drug use is in the top three most prevalent activities of tourists along with gambling and sex. A look at the Crime Map shows very few drug related arrests. However, **Nevada is known for having the harshest penalties for drug offenders in the country**.

The drug use is very difficult to control; however, the laws are enforced whenever possible. If a person is caught with drugs in a typical pat down for entrance into clubs or pool parties, Metro Police will be called and the offender will get a peek at the inside of the Las Vegas jail. At that point, an attorney is required. See Appendix F Attorneys, or Appendix B Laws and Ordinances for a more detailed description of various laws.

In a recent documentary on drugs in Sin City, a dealer indicated that roughly 60% of people coming to Las Vegas come for drugs. Drugs are easy to find, and generally, much of the drug use occurs in the entertainment clubs. The type of club and the music that is offered is an indicator of the types of drugs available. The drug dictionary indicated that the most used letter for illegal drugs was "S," totaling 304.

"According to Nevada law, it is illegal to import, transport, exchange, barter, supply, prescribe, dispense, give away, administer, or manufacture" any controlled substance. Drug sales can be charged as drug trafficking if more than four grams (the weight of a nickel is 5 grams) of a Schedule I drug was involved or 28 grams or more of a Schedule II drug."

"Under Nevada law, a person can be charged with possessing a controlled substance or trafficking in a controlled substance in a variety of ways. Possession includes not only having direct physical control over a thing at a given time (actual possession), but also includes constructive possession which involves a person who, although not in actual possession, knowingly has both the power and the intention to exercise control over the drug either directly or through another person. Possession can also be sole or joint. This means that under certain circumstances, multiple people can be charged with possessing the same drugs in question."

How big is the drug industry in Las Vegas? A quick back of the envelope calculation (see Appendix D) indicates that it is a $7.5 to $14 billion dollar industry for cocaine and marijuana alone, and that amount might even double when including ecstasy, amphetamines, designer drugs and illegal prescription drugs. The Las Vegas Valley has approximately 2.5 million residents, so this equates to over $3,000 per resident.

FINDING AN ATTORNEY

If one gets in trouble with the law, especially while engaging in adult activities in Las Vegas, the name and phone number of a local attorney will be helpful. See Appendix F Attorneys for a list of attorneys that work with sex, drug, driving, and gun related crimes in Las Vegas. Each of the attorneys listed have very instructive "must read" web pages that give fairly clear guidelines relating to City, County, and State laws. A complete list of Las Vegas attorneys is available on-line.

There are a few attorneys that have very informative web pages that provide excellent coverage of many of the common laws that tourists are arrested for in Las Vegas. It is fun to take a few minutes and look at each website for a glimpse of the legal side of Las Vegas.

Potter Law Offices

Brown Law Offices

Law Office of Chip Siegel

Law Office of Joel M. Mann

For specific information on some Laws and Ordinances, see Appendix B Laws and Ordinances.

Now that we have covered some of the laws and how to stay out of trouble, let's look at adult entertainment in Las Vegas and find out where people go for fun.

6

ENTERTAINMENT CLUBS

L as Vegas is the city of clubs. Finding a club that meets your fancy may seem confusing at first, so the following should help narrow down the choices. Some advice when visiting Las Vegas for the first time is to keep your options open, spend your first night checking out the different scenes, and then narrow it down to where you want to spend your time. For local information What's-On (shows), Las Vegas Weekly (nightlife), Las Vegas Magazine (entertainment, Seven Magazine (general), and Inside Henderson Magazine (Henderson and greater area) all provide excellent current information. Las Vegas Advisor is also a very good Las Vegas website that covers most interests.

ENTERTAINMENT CLUBS

There are a number of entertainment clubs in Las Vegas that provide an array of music and dancing with top DJ's and live bands to meet the fancy of nearly every adult age group. These clubs serve alcohol and are therefore limited to adults over 21. Many clubs will have a celebrity seated at a conspicuous table to encourage patrons to text or tweet friends about the "who" they are in the same club with. Visit the club blogs to see who was recently spotted partying at which club.

One of the highest grossing clubs in Las Vegas is Pure at Caesar's Palace. Pure grossed over $430 million in 2013. It was bought by Hakkasan Group and closed recently for renovation and is scheduled to reopen in early 2015.

A similar club, Hakkasan Night Club, located at the MGM Grand, run by Angel Management, is gaining a good reputation. On-line tickets start at $10 for women and $20 for males.

Another well-known nightspot is the <u>Light Nightclub</u> at the Mandalay Bay. Tickets start at $20 for females and $40 for male patrons.

For a complete list of clubs, visit <u>entertainment clubs</u> on the Las Vegas website.

Las Vegas clubs commonly require a cover charge and the drinks are pricey. A typical VIP table is the price of a bottle ($375). A good rule of thumb is 17 shots in a bottle; so, a $375 bottle is equivalent to $22 a drink. If your group is going to consume at least 17 drinks, you will most likely save money purchasing a bottle. Figure $100 for a lap dance.

Admission for women is usually reduced, and in some clubs the ladies are admitted free. These clubs tend to support intermingling and are typically good places to meet members of the opposite sex. The music, code words, atmosphere, appearance, and character of the crowd usually impart a glimpse into the demeanor of the scene. If you don't feel comfortable, you are probably in the wrong venue.

Drug use in clubs is frowned upon. Bags are searched and men are patted down. Caution is advised as Nevada has the toughest drug laws in the nation. With that being said, those that are into drugs will find plenty of like-minded people; keep in mind that the drugs of choice are typically associated with the music that is offered.

CLUB REVIEWS

There are a number of popular clubs to investigate and it is worthwhile to look over the reviews before going to a club. One of the more up-to-date review sites is <u>Yelp's Strip Club Las Vegas</u>. <u>Bachelor Vegas</u> also has some good current reviews of strip clubs.

An excellent review site that covers strip clubs is <u>Naughty Reviews</u>. You will need to register to join the site, so if you're worried about security, now is the time to use the temporary email address created just for your Las Vegas trip. This website is very good and provides detailed information and excellent reviews about the inside operations.

A good general website for nightlife in Las Vegas is the Vegas Travel Site. This is an excellent top-level introduction to nightlife in Las Vegas.

In addition, the VIP service businesses discussed in the VIP Services chapter typically promote clubs where they know their clients will be pleased. Some clubs that are not in the headlines but have high review ratings from a variety of websites are promoted by these service businesses.

For example, Galavantier Las Vegas shows the following clubs with high scores: Light Nightclub (90) at the Mandalay Bay, Surrender Nightclub (89), Tryst Nightclub (92), and XS Nightclub (94) all three at the Wynn, and Body English (80) at the Hard Rock Hotel and Casino. Something different is VIP Club Crawl (90), a service that specializes in taking customers around to a number of clubs in one night.

These clubs might be missed in the clutter of all the high paid advertising that a tourist in Las Vegas must weed through in order to find something of interest. It is worthwhile to spend some time shopping around to learn more about all the different clubs. A daytime visit to a club can be most productive to get the layout and to see how things work.

A good recommendation after selecting a club to visit is to look at the negative reviews for the club because management and staff changes can significantly affect the positive atmosphere of an establishment.

To do a Google search on a club, type into Google *"(club name) negative reviews"* or *"negative reviews (club name)"* An example is "negative reviews sapphire." These reviews provide plenty of detail on what to avoid and what bothered people about the place. One example of a useful "heads up" was a $60 charge at an ATM machine for $300 cash--a rip-off 20% fee. This is nice knowledge to have before going into a club.

STRIP CLUB ETIQUETTE

Before embarking on a tour of strip clubs, a quick review of Strip

Club Etiquette will provide some highly recommended behavioral rules. It is a "*must read*" site.

FUNNY MONEY

If you want to tip the workers at the clubs, you generally should pay with cash. If you want to use a credit card, you must purchase "Funny Money" (chips), which adds an automatic 20% charge on your card. You can buy more if you like; however, chips cannot be returned. You cannot cash the chips back in and cannot buy drinks with them. Better to have the cash ahead of time.

The cocktail waitresses are employees of the clubs and depend highly on tips for income. A general practice is 20%, however many girls have to work hard to get anywhere near this amount. There are over 3,000 cocktail servers in the local union. Many are making minimum wage, so tips are the major part of their income. With 10 clubs running with over 250 to 500 girls per club on average, there are somewhere between 2,500 to 5,000 strippers working the club floors on weekends. Most strippers have to pay the clubs to work there and work as independent contractors. You should keep this in mind when you are tipping in any entertainment club.

ATM MACHINES

Obtain cash first before going into clubs. The ATM fees are on the order of 15% inside clubs and some clubs are known for exorbitant fees.

GENTLEMEN'S CLUBS AND CLUBS FOR WOMEN

Gentlemen's clubs fall into two categories: topless and totally nude. Topless clubs serve alcohol and are restricted to adults over 21. Alcohol is not served in the nude clubs and these clubs tend to be a big attraction for the 18 to 21 year olds. The only exception to this rule is the Palomino Club in North Las Vegas, the only totally nude club allowed to serve alcoholic beverages.

Club Viva Las Vegas offers multi-club packages for their Top 10 listed clubs. Up to four clubs can be visited in one night with limo transportation provided as part of the package.

A growing number of these gentlemen's clubs now feature male entertainment just for women. Club Viva offers Bachelor and Bachelorette parties, VIP services, large group specials, as well as deals for couples.

TOPLESS CLUBS OR STRIP CLUBS

Big draws to Las Vegas are the gentleman's clubs, or strip clubs, which next to gaming are the second largest earnings entertainment businesses in Las Vegas. Before embarking on a night out on the town, take some time to visit informative web and review sites to ensure a more exciting stay in Las Vegas.

Spearmint Rhino is one of the better-known clubs in Las Vegas; it features a very dark atmosphere, so be aware that it may take time to acclimate. The club has been popular in Las Vegas for a number of years. The well-designed layout has a prominent center stage with supporting table stages where as many as 200 dancers show off their physical features and talents. It should be easy to find the girl of your dreams somewhere in this club.

Drinks are expensive. Daytime hours might be a little cheaper. Ladies can only attend with a male escort and are not allowed to mingle with customers. One exception, if a group of ladies wants to go in, they will make a special case, no mingling however. There are a number of special packages available that include free cover charge, and discounted VIP entry and limousine pickup.

Cheetahs features over 500 girls everyday, and is one of the largest strip clubs in Las Vegas. This club is worth a daytime visit for a quick tour to get your bearings for your visit later in the evening.

Club Paradise offers gorgeous women dressed in sexy gowns performing choreographed shows. The setting is not as intimate as other clubs, so getting special lap dances becomes a little more difficult.

Olympic Garden (OG) Gentlemen's Club, located at the north end of the Strip, is separated with men downstairs and ladies upstairs. The cover charge is steep at $30 and the reviews are mixed. The upstairs club has some good <u>reviews</u> compared to some not so good ones for the downstairs club.

NUDE CLUBS

<u>Little Darlings</u> is an extraordinary nightspot at the north end of the Strip; it is known by the locals as Little D's. Located just off Western and Industrial, this totally nude club will not disappoint anyone over 18.

The club hosts a large main stage with plenty of seating, and features over 125 gorgeous girls per day. The entrance fee is $10 for locals and $30 for out-of-state. The silver package, at $150, includes a VIP booth and free limousine pickup from your hotel. You will probably have to take a cab back.

You can also get a bed dance as compared to a lap dance. There are around 20 private rooms with beds. For $20 you can lie on your back and have a lady wiggle and waggle, twist and jiggle, or squirm and worm on top of you for the three-minute duration of a song. How personal you get depends on how the money flows (how many dances you buy and how much you tip) and your personal hygiene.

Hint: After a few bed dances you may want to go over to Wells Spa on Convention Drive and get a body shampoo to clean up a bit, relax, and have a better chance for a pleasant surprise with a beautiful lady.

What do 18 to 21 year olds do in Las Vegas? Since they cannot legally gamble or drink, Little D's is the local hangout for the younger crowd. It's a great initiation place and a guaranteed fun spot for everyone over 18 visiting Las Vegas. Ladies under the age of 21 can work here and most of the strippers are 18-21 years old. So if you want to spend a few hours goggling at young naked bodies, this is the place.

Here is a good review from <u>The Wizard Of Vegas</u> that is well written, relevant, and worth the read. The Wizard of Vegas website is a very good place to spend some time learning more about Las Vegas. The site is geared more for gambling, but also has good information on hotels and clubs.

LADIES CLUBS

Sapphire Gentlemen's Club will host a decent bachelor party for men; however, the club is becoming better known for the Men of Sapphire and the wild and memorable bachelorette parties. The club is huge and is known for employing the most dancers in Las Vegas. The main showroom is a full 15,000 square feet with a multilevel center stage that has unique rent by the hour skyboxes for excellent viewing of the dancers.

Chippendales The Show, located in the Rio, will make any lady happy, and for a fun time afterwards visit the Voodoo Steak And Rooftop Nightclub. The nightclub has one of the best views of the Las Vegas Strip and is the perfect place for a proposal.

Thunder from Down Under at the Excalibur is a big draw "ladies only" show guaranteed to provide top-notch entertainment.

POOL PARTIES

The venues in Las Vegas are continually changing to accommodate the shifting needs of the transient Las Vegas society. A recent USA Today article "Adult and topless pools continue to make waves" suggests that topless pool parties in Las Vegas are still a top attraction and a must see activity. Pool parties at the top of the list (from VIP service companies) are Azure Pool Lounge and Tao Beach at The Palazzo. Also included are Bare Pool Lounge at the Mirage, and the Daylight Beach Club at Mandalay Bay. Hotel pools change in popularity from season to season, so before booking read the current positive and negative reviews.

POOL CLUBS

If you want to try something new that you may not be able to do at home, try The Topless in Las Vegas for a more private poolside affair. If warm weather and swimming pools stir your adrenaline, then you might want to start with a Google search for cool pools to find the most recent information on swimming pools in Las Vegas.

It may be difficult to spy nude ladies around the public Las Vegas pools; however, there are other more private avenues to connect with locals that have no problem getting rid of the bathing suits. Check out the "Meetup" website and look for Nude Sunbathing in Las Vegas.

SEX IN THE CLUBS

Finding sex in the clubs is not difficult, but it takes a bit of patience and finesse. The first requirement is money. When you pass $100 bills around, it gets people's attention.

The second most important action is to impress the right people. The dancer, the bouncer, and the house should be on the top of the list to impress.

Impressing the house, the bouncer, and the dancer are easy if you possesses one of those no limit credit cards like the American Express "BLACK" Centurion Card, especially if $1,000 in Funny Money is purchased upon entrance into a club.

Dancers love to see the money, so once that is established, you can create a bit more interest. Chances are if you have good personal hygiene, have recently bathed, have used a little deodorant, and have a clean fresh mouth then you are on your way to 2nd base.

When it comes to dancers, the *"rule"* is *"**don't touch**;"* so let the ladies lead the way. When you think things look good, go for the VIP room. The dancer will be splitting some of the dough with the bouncer, which allows a little more freedom.

A legal prostitute gets about $1,000 an hour, so if the dancer thinks her VIP guest will turn loose of 10 or 20 Ben's, then chances might be good for a date when she gets off work. But remember that it is always just a chance, and not a guarantee.

If a girl hops onto your lap and starts doing a lap dance without asking, it is time to let her know the lap dance is not wanted. She cannot charge for an unwanted dance. In order to be paid, the girls need to ask if you want to continue into a second dance (if a first has already been agreed upon).

If the chance encounter in Las Vegas somehow leads to a limousine, a $100 tip to the driver should buy more than enough privacy for personal desires. See Appendix G for a few smart phone people finder apps.

GAY CLUBS AND BARS

Las Vegas is well known for its gay, lesbian, bisexual, and transgendered (GLBT) community along with the clubs, bars, and hotels that make such a community so interesting. The official Vegas travel site has a respectable listing for many Las Vegas GLBT bars, clubs, and pool clubs enjoyed by the entire community. Las Vegas Gay Bars Guide - Best Gay Nightlife in Las Vegas is an excellent summary of the current gay bars and clubs in Las Vegas.

There are two well-known gay areas in Las Vegas. One is the Gay Quarter that runs along Paradise north of the airport to the Hard Rock Hotel that sports over a dozen gay bars. The other is the Commercial Center that can be looked down upon from the Stratosphere, along the 900 block of E. Sahara when looking toward McCarran airport.

This center, at first glance, might look like a seedy area of town, but the Crime Map of the area shows the north side of the Las Vegas Country Club to be relatively calm. Because of the tourist volume, the police department patrols this area relatively well at night. Check the crime map first before going.

Three gay bars continually top the list on websites: One is The Garage at 1487 East Flamingo Road just east of the University of Nevada Las Vegas; another is the famous Drink and Drag on Fremont Street, and nearby in Old Las Vegas is Snicks Place, one of the oldest gay bars in Las Vegas. All three are worth visiting to see and experience the atmosphere of a gay bar in the loose setting of Las Vegas. Other notable clubs are Share and Piranha Nightclubs.

Las Vegas at Vegas.com includes a good review of gay bars; in addition, there are complete planning tools for the GLBT community. Las Vegas admits to being gay friendly.

7
VIP SERVICES

A number of VIP Services operate in Las Vegas, and they offer many different packages. These service companies can provide as little as a limo ride, up to complete reservation and booking services, including a special escort service to bypass entrance lines at clubs.

VIP service suppliers are built around good contacts in Las Vegas and have special relationships with clubs for excellent tables. Regularly bringing paying customers to clubs establishes the good relationship, and thus the benefits found with VIP services are not available any other way.

Many clubs offer a VIP line bypass, but the tables that are offered may not be in good areas. A good VIP service will provide beginning to end service for a fun night out, including transportation, jumping lines, obtaining good tables, providing interference when needed to ward off aggressive men (for their female clients), and making sure clients are not getting cheated. They will even watch the ladies purses while they are dancing.

VIP services normally require up-front payments with a credit card to ensure the premium service that clients expect.

One specialized VIP service is offered by Robert Sheets via his business, SheetsVIP. Robert offers a personal premium hosting service to boost his clients hourly cost/benefit return. He personally looks after clients' needs ensuring a safe, enjoyable stay in Las Vegas. If one wants to have a fast pace, exclusive, high-class time in Las Vegas at reasonable prices, SheetsVIP is one of Las Vegas' up and coming performers that won't disappoint. Sheets VIP is also found on Facebook.

Galavantier Las Vegas is another VIP service that offers a broad array of packages that boast an extensive list of fun time tours, parties, outdoor activities, and nightlife in and around Las Vegas.

Some VIP services only offer services to and from clubs with preferential seating and immediate club entry. Club Viva Las Vegas is one such service.

Other well-known VIP service companies are Red Carpet VIP, Vegas VIP, and Vegas Inside Players.

These VIP service companies keep up to date on the hottest places and the newest events in the Las Vegas scene, and their websites are excellent places to look for a quick glimpse of Las Vegas. One should keep in mind that if a club has a low rating or their service is bad, a VIP service will drop it, or it will demand a refund or compensation for its customers.

The VIP companies must uphold their reputation, which is dependent upon good client service, so they want their clients to be pleased. As with any business in Las Vegas, it is good to shop around.

8
GAMBLING

Many people come to Las Vegas to gamble with the hopes of striking it rich. Most of these people go home with empty pockets and wonder, "What the hell happened?"

GAMBLING PLAN

If you are going to play the slot machines, or any other gambling game in Las Vegas, it is advised to have a plan to follow to keep out of financial trouble. Here is an example of a plan that will ensure that you will not overspend and will go home with cash in your pockets. In addition, this plan ensures you will not be going away ashamed or disappointed in your behavior. If it is a slot machine you are playing, "always," set the machine for "max bet" to maximize your chances. Play the "highest denomination" that you can afford, as these machines pay back at a higher percentage.

1. Set a daily gambling budget for your stay; example might be $100 a day.

2. Put $100 into a separate envelope for each day and put these into the hotel room safe.

3. On day one, pull out the first envelope and put the money into the left pocket for men or a separate purse pocket for women.

4. Set a betting limit. This might be $0.25 for a quarter slot machine.

5. When you win, get your cash slip, and put it in your pocket, even if it is only for $0.25.

6. Put the winnings into your right pocket or separate purse pocket.

7. Take a breather.

8. Go back to the game and use betting money from your left pocket, etc.

9. When you are out of money in the left pocket you are done for the day. Take your cash slips (right pocket) to a kiosk and cash them in. Take your winnings back to your hotel safe and keep them in your envelope for the day.

10. Next day, take out envelope #2 and continue.

When you go home, you can tell everyone you WON in Las Vegas, and you will know exactly how much you made.

What you gain from this process is the ability to GET UP FROM THE SLOT MACHINE and go cash out as compared to STAYING until you are OUT OF MONEY, including all the money you won but rolled over into playing at the machine. The machines in Las Vegas are programmed to eventually win all the money that is put into them. So the shorter the time you stay at a machine, the greater your chances of winning something more than what you put in.

Here is a typical example: You go out for dinner and your spouse wants to bet one dollar in a quarter slot machine. You insert your player's card into the machine. You set the machine at max bet. You play your first quarter. The first quarter is a loss; the next quarter wins $1.00. At that point, you cash out, take the slip to the kiosk, and get $1.00 in winnings plus the $0.50 you did not spend. You go away with $1.50 and that is it. You feel great having beat the "one arm bandit" and go home with a 50% gain. If you are on the envelope system, you can then go back to your favorite machine or try another and continue the process until your left pocket is depleted.

This compares to a friend that came to town. She was playing the slot machines. When asked if she won anything, her reply was, "Well, no I lost." Next question was, "How much did you lose?" She replied, "Well, umm, I lost $200." I then asked, "Did you have a plan and how did you feel?" She replied in a low voice, "Nope!" She was upset with herself for not having any control over the game.

Recently I was able to watch a professional gambler play the slots. He had several thousand dollars in $100 bills in his hand. He inserted his player's card and set the slot dollar machine for max bet. He put in a $100 and pushed the buttons several times and then he won some money. He cashed out with $175. He inserted another $100 bill, pushed the button, and immediately won. He cashed out and put the $135 ticket in his pocket. He inserted another $100 bill and pushed the button repeatedly until he lost it all. He inserted another $100 bill, repeated the process winning $125, cashed out, and put the ticket in his pocket. After he went though the pile of money in his left hand at several machines, he quit. He cashed out all the tickets and showed that he made about 50% on his money. His secret was to limit his time at the machine by cashing out every time he won. He always won and never, ever, lost all that he had. He explained that he had some $50K winnings, and some terrible losses, but he never went home a loser of everything. The author has personally seen his 1099's for over $100,000 two years in a row. He has fun, limits his losses with a plan, and occasionally wins big. Year over year he continually makes money.

FEELING GOOD ABOUT YOURSELF

If you want to go home feeling good about yourself, do the following:

1. Set a limit for gambling. The amount depends on your personal budget, but always set a limit that is within reasonable means.

2. Have a plan on how you are going to operate, such as the methodology above.

3. Stick to the limit and the plan.

4. Use your player's card or preferred card for the casino you are in. If you don't have one, register and get one because it is free and they have many benefits.

5. Cash out your winnings on a regular basis.

Here is a rule of thumb to keep in mind — the easier a game is to play, the worse the odds. Before you put one cent into a machine, have a plan. Below are some commandments and rules developed by people that have spent considerable time at the gaming tables.

The Wizard of Odds really stands out as a complete website with information on gambling, including the odds and rules, as well as video tutorials. The Wizard of Vegas is also a very well done website that is geared to the gambler in Las Vegas. In addition, the author includes reviews on hotels and even shows some trail maps for those that want to get out for a little exercise. If you are coming to Las Vegas to gamble, this website should be included as a must read.

The Wizard of Odds also lists The Ten Commandments of Gambling, all of which are worth following:

1. Thou shalt not cheat

2. Thou shalt honor thy gambling debts

3. Thou shalt expect to lose

4. Thou shalt trust the odds, not hunches

5. Thou shalt not over bet thy bankroll

6. Thou shalt not believe in betting systems

7. Thou shalt not hedge thy bet

8. Thou shalt covet good rules

9. Thou shalt not make side bets

10. Thou shalt have good gambling etiquette

Another set of invaluable rules to abide by when in Las Vegas are the Casino Guide rules:

1. Don't Gamble Drunk

2. Don't get caught cheating

3. Use your player's card

4. Don't Swear/Cuss

5. Tip Fairly

6. Pay attention
7. Don't forget to redeem your tickets/chips
8. Have a goal in mind
9. Bet for the dealer
10. Don't give away points
11. Don't play tired or sleepy
12. Don't critique the play of others
13. Don't blow smoke into people's faces
14. Don't play for comps
15. Don't bring kids to gamble

For those first timers that are excited about gambling and are looking forward to the game, many hotels offer free lessons in a non-intimidating environment; they are worth exploring. You can learn in a casual atmosphere with low stakes and then, when comfortable, move off on your own to bet within your stakes at the game of your choice. Good Luck!

9
SEX IN LAS VEGAS

Many people visit Las Vegas for conferences, and a big enticement to get people to come to the conferences are the extracurricular activities that the city has to offer. On top of the list are most of the well-known vices such as drinking, smoking, gambling, drugs, and sex. In addition, people are drawn to the extravagant Cirque shows and the close by natural wonders of the world that surround Las Vegas, such as the Grand Canyon, Zion Park, the Hoover Dam, and Death Valley.

The unspoken top of the list, however, is sex. Las Vegas is the only place in the United States where any person so inclined is assured of *"getting laid."* Whether you want to interact with live girls on high speed Internet, watch endless adult movies in the privacy of your hotel room, hire cheap hookers, or spend $1,000 to $2,000 an hour on bucket list prostitutes or escorts, Las Vegas has all you desire.

Just a quick reminder, if your spouse is going to ask what you did in Las Vegas, perhaps a visit to a museum or two, listed in Chapter 17, would be wise. Picking up some novelty souvenirs will make the conversation even less strenuous. Everything you want is here in Las Vegas!

LEGAL REMINDERS

Over the years law enforcement and legislators appear to have tried to legally interrupt prostitution in the city of Las Vegas only to see the laws stuck down. Everything from handouts on the streets, to rolling billboards, to web page advertisements, to newspapers ads, and to personals on the web have held up in court via first amendment and other rights. The right to dance is considered an art form, and hiring an escort is legal.

In the end, law enforcement works in the areas where it is most effective with limited resources. It tries to keep the street hookers on the edge, so that the worst part of the trade is not as openly conspicuous. That is where most of the arrests are made. Even so, many of the arrests are made not for sex related crimes, but for disturbing the peace, loitering, trespassing, or misuse of drugs and alcohol.

If one looks at the Las Vegas crime map, there are almost no [SC] "Sex Crimes" shown, however there are plenty of "Disturbing The Peace" crimes, many of which are likely a hooker who is taken off the street for a few hours.

The only ladies legal to be in a hotel room for sex are 18 years or older and are considered consenting adults (not a prostitute soliciting money for sex), or an escort (dispatched to your room) who must be 21 years or older, registered and carrying an Escort Card. Escorts cannot legally solicit money for sex, however, the charge for escort time is considered by many to be all-inclusive. One way of protecting yourself is to insist that the escort show their Escort Card. That means he/she is registered and over 21 years old.

Any lady that approaches a man at the bar other than a happy consenting adult also looking for a good time is a prostitute or an escort. Therefore, if the lady asks, "Would you like to go for a ride?" Your response is, "Do you have a card?" If she has a card, take a good look at it (taking a smart phone photo of it might also be appropriate). At this point, the negotiation is for TIME not SEX.

For an example of a worst-case scenario, imagine this: A nice lady comes up to the bar next to you and engages in interesting conversation. You offer to buy a drink. She quickly leads you believe she is willing to have sex for money. You agree and negotiate a price. She turns out to be 17 years old and a vice cop pulls out his or her badge. You have been negotiating for sex – prostitution (illegal), with a minor (really bad), and you bought her an alcoholic drink (contributing to delinquency of a minor). You are hauled off to jail.

By being informed and aware of what to expect and how to behave, you can avoid being arrested. Be aware that it is *"legal"* for police officers to engage in illegal activities while doing stings on prostitution. This means they may have fake IDs, airplane tickets, and hotel rooms set up especially for the sting operation. Normally these are set up to nail prostitutes and pimps. It makes little sense for the Metro Police to set up false fronts and advertise with false numbers to nail tourists. The tourist industry would decline rapidly as the word spread. 10 Girls to Avoid in Las Vegas is a good article to glance over before launching a hunt.

The current prostitution operation in Las Vegas might be classified as a typical RICO (Racketeer Influenced and Corrupt Organizations Act) business in the practice of committing crimes. Prosecution takes a U.S. Attorney and a lot of manpower and time to convict. The city of Las Vegas does not have the capability to go after these operations without federal help, and the feds are typically going after bigger fish.

Prostitution in Las Vegas is easy to place at international crime levels involving groups from foreign countries, but remains low on the crime list because of low violence and little media attention. This article is a very interesting read and shows the difficulty in shutting down illegal sex operations in Las Vegas: Sex Industry Put On Notice.

Prostitution used to be arranged through the bell desks in the major hotels, but the practice took a big hit in the 1980s when the Las Vegas Hilton was busted. However, the practice of workers helping customers find what they are looking for still thrives today. If one is discrete, hotel employees (who depend on tips) will make sure that a customer's needs are met. It may be as easy as slipping a bartender a twenty and asking where you can find a pretty lady, or a nice gentleman, for some company.

HOTELS

Sex in Las Vegas is normally between consensual adults, with an escort (sex is not negotiated), or a prostitute (where sex is negotiated and is against the law). All of these relationships will normally occur in a hotel room. Sex can also occur in the back of a limousine, which is becoming a fashionable practice.

It is wise for persons that are engaging in sexual activities in their hotel room to understand some of the risks involved. Opening the door to one's hotel room invites the unknown guest into close enough proximity to personal valuables that theft is relatively easy.

To protect personal affects from being stolen, the room safe is one of the best places to store valuables out of easy reach. Valuables include personal computers, watches, wallets, cell phones, car keys, cash, and anything else of importance. It is suggested that you even put the hotel soap, conditioner, shampoo, and other bathroom essentials out of reach. Assume that your temporary guest has real sticky fingers and that if it isn't bolted down, it will be lifted. It is suggested to have only the cash needed for the transaction available.

How about room keys? Getting your second electronic room key lifted leaves your room accessible to unwanted entry later on. If in doubt, get your room rekeyed. If you don't have enough space in your safe, call the hotel desk and see if they can hold your valuables.

Disabled men, especially those in wheel chairs, are easy prey for prostitutes. Disabled persons get the same attention as a rock star when it comes to prostitutes, and prostitutes consider them easy pickings. Disabled men need to be much more vigilant and protective of personal items in a hotel room.

WEB CAMS

Of course, if one is skittish on inviting an escort to their hotel room, there is always the option of using the Internet for virtual sex. HD Live Web Cams are only one of the latest developments in the sex industry. An interesting article to read is "<u>Ten indispensible technologies built by the pornography industry</u>," which describes ten of the current technologies that we enjoy every day that many would never have guessed were driven by the pornographic industry.

"Porn: The Hidden Engine That Drives Innovation In Tech" is an excellent article on how pornography generated many high speed and high bandwidth technologies for web cams. This is amazing stuff to comprehend, and now one can freely browse and visit with all sorts of ladies via live web cams. It doesn't take much imagination to visualize "reach out and touch someone" technology being right around the corner.

ESCORTS — OUT-CALL AND IN-CALL

Prostitution is illegal in Clark County and that includes the city of Las Vegas and the Las Vegas Metropolitan area. However, escorts and entertainers are legal and most of the sex in Las Vegas falls in this arena. These services are typically found as Escorts that will work out-call (to your location) or in-call (you go to their location). Massage may also be listed for out-call or in-call.

Generally, sex is included in the price and is not negotiated. You may see signs or instructions that read, "Kindly prepare donations in an envelope with my name on it and properly place within view for me to see. There will be NO form of discussion about money during our encounter. Thanks in Advance. Rate: 1 hr.-$500, 2 hr.-$900, 3 hr.-$1200, 4 hr.-$1600."

There are many ladies of the night available in Las Vegas and it is quite easy to look at reviews for each of them as you would for any other entertainment venue. One website, Naughty Reviews (Escorts) (Female) lists female escorts for men and Naughty Reviews (Escorts) (Male) lists male escorts for women. In all, Naughty Reviews lists over 1900 escorts. A premium status (3 days for $4.99) allows one to read all the reviews. They include information such as explicit details of the escort service provided and how much was paid, including tip. The free browsing provides limited access to reviews.

Here is a small summary of the Naughty Reviews website:

Female Escorts

 There are over 2,000 escorts listed. Many of the female escorts indicate they have ID Verification, however some

do not. Prices ranged from $150 for a ½ hour to $250 for 1 hour. Most likely a tip would be appreciated, even expected.

Escort Agencies

There are over 90 Escort Agencies listed. The process would be to call the agency, indicate what type of escort one would like, and they will advise as to how much. The escorts will most likely come to the requester's hotel room. Prices ranged from $200 for ½ hour to $500 for an hour if the escort carries a card, and as low as $150 if they do not have a card. Tips for extra services would most likely apply. Some take credit cards and some do not.

It is advised that the requestor write down the name of the agent talked with along with the phone number. A good check is to call the agency back and request the dispatcher for verification. Taking a photo of the escort's card before making payment is a good practice.

Shemale Escorts

There are 11 shemale escorts listed on Naughty Reviews. In some instances, these are listed as TS or transsexual. Some allow for messages via the website. Prices range from $80 for ½ hour to $300 for an hour, no ID.

Some escorts on this website indicate they have "ID Verification," which means that they should show their escort cards if asked.

Male Escorts for Ladies

Cowboys 4 Angels is the place for women, or "cougars," to find and enjoy the company of quality male escorts. A particular cowboy (a well-dressed, good-looking man, in good shape, and who professes to live a healthy lifestyle) might just be the ticket for an evening out on the town. Cowboys 4 Angels is a higher quality website that provides for the needs of ladies that have money to spend. Also, see the section under Personals below, especially if a woman is looking for the man of her dreams.

Street Cards

Cards are freely handed out to anyone and everyone walking down the Strip or near the Las Vegas convention center. These cards are for escort service call centers or agencies and are avenues for under aged prostitutes and prostitutes working with gangs or pimps. The girls that show up to the caller's hotel room will not look at all like the photo on the card.

When the number on the card is called, the agency will ask what type of girl is wanted, such as nationality and hair color and sometimes even more specific details, and will quote a rate. This is the agency rate. Usually the girl makes nothing, or only a small fraction of this rate. The caller must provide a phone number and a hotel room number. When the call is terminated, the agency will then call back to make sure the same person answers. The girl will then be dispatched to the room.

When the girl arrives, she usually phones the call center to report that she is with the client, which starts the clock. The girl will request the agency fee up front, and then she negotiates the service (if it is for sex it is illegal) and the price, which is above the rate quoted by the agency. At the same time, the girl will be scoping out the room for anything that can be easily ripped off. She will want the money in advance. No tip included, this is the full price, unless in the middle of the fun she indicates she can provide more excitement for more money.

When she is done, she will usually leave the client in bed and excuse herself to the bathroom to clean up, where she will collect any of the amenities supplied by the hotel and deposit them in her purse. Hopefully the caller has been smart enough to clean out the bathroom and has deposited personal valuables (including wallet) in the room or hotel safe. The article Prostitution in Las Vegas describes the risks of this venue for finding a prostitute. There is little recourse that patrons have with this type of escort if the experience is poor. It is better to go to a website, such as Naughty Reviews above, where you have the option of writing a review about your experience. If a girl has an ID card, you can report any theft to the police and to the agency.

Chinese Newspapers

Recently Las Vegas has been catering more and more to the Chinese adult customer. An interesting process to find out-call girls is to go to Chinatown and pick up one of the Chinese newspapers. Find the pages with sexy girls and phone numbers; these are out-call numbers run by a call agency, most likely Chinese owned.

If you call one of these numbers and ask about a massage, they will ask the caller if they know Chinese. If response is "No" they may hang up. If the caller instead says that their Chinese friend recommended this number then they will be happy to discuss the services offered.

One can ask for girls of many different nationalities including Russian, Chinese, Japanese, or Latino. The agency will provide the caller with the price for whatever service they are interested in. These out-call girls most likely will not be licensed escorts. They may, however, be outcall massage providers.

The police are not able to read Chinese and therefore are unable to know what the ads are explicitly advertising. Like any of the out-call agencies, out-call girls may be underage, so the consumer must beware. It would be best to specify over 21 with an escort ID.

Escorts and Massage – Independents

Escort services are moving to the web to maintain privacy and to gain distance from law enforcement scrutiny. The Eros Guide Las Vegas is one location where many independents advertise. Their services range from escorts to massage to Tantra massage (which tends to confuse Tantric bliss with ordinary orgasmic pleasure). This site is straightforward and provides contact information such as web pages with phone numbers, and includes an assortment of pictures of escorts. The photos of the service providers are usually of the escort, so you get what you see. Communication is direct with the escort. VIP escorts tend to be more beautiful and more experienced, and as expected will cost more.

City Vibe is another interesting website for independents. This site includes pictures, contact information, and videos of escorts. This website has been in business for a number of years. This site introduces some stunning escorts. For example: If a man were looking for a perfect rendezvous, a <u>Blond Russian Knockout</u> straight out of a James Bond movie just might be the ticket for the evening.

From this web advertisement page, one can click to the lady's <u>personal website</u> for some awesome pictures and personal videos. If one would like to see the reviews for this lady, these can be found at <u>Adultfax Review</u> listed under external links on her City Vibe web page.

This is where one may want to use a temporary email address. The review page is extensive and lists the service provider's appearance, and the detailed services provided. This "Blond Russian Knockout" escort will cost $2,000 for two hours and $3,200 for an escort/dinner date. She rates 9 on appearance and performance. Wouldn't this be a nice birthday present?

If VIP ladies are too expensive, another straightforward website with over 370 escorts listed by name is Las Vegas Free Exotic Vegas Escort Reviews - <u>LVFever</u>. This is a free site and registration allows one to access reviews, which not only list the escorts by name, but also provide contact information. It is easy for one to select a lady with a good review, make an easy click to check out her web page, and then call or email her.

If you are not totally worn out looking at escort sites, <u>The Erotic Review</u> is a worldwide site and specializes in escorts. Here is an example of an <u>available escort</u>, which was randomly picked from the front page of the reviews as it came up. Here is <u>her personal web page</u>. A look at her rate page showed $500/hour, 5 hours $1700, Overnight $2500, or one day $3000.

<u>Las Vegas Escort Prices</u> are reviewed in this Las Vegas article along with some good rip-off information.

Limousine Services

Only in Las Vegas might one be able to rent a limousine that caters to sexual experiences. A limousine can be leased to provide transportation to and from different adult venues in the city. One such service is <u>Las Vegas Limo Diaries</u>, which caters to nearly every experience including escorts such as <u>One More Sin Escorts</u>, a service that will provide quality escorts at going rates. Just about every kind of escort required to meet a person's needs is available on this website. This limousine service also includes <u>brothel options</u> in Pahrump, NV.

Personals

On-line personals have become one method for prostitutes and in-call businesses to advertise their services in Las Vegas.

<u>Craigslist</u> has a personal page for individuals that are seeking relationships; some are looking to connect in Las Vegas. "Adult Services" on Craigslist for Las Vegas was recently shutdown, but the activities seem to have shifted to <u>Therapeutic Services</u>. Male therapists offering massage services for females are listed along with plenty of services offered by female and male therapists. Photos of the therapists are generally supplied. For better massage parlor information, see the Massage Parlors and Spas section below.

<u>Back Page</u> offers many personal adult services in Las Vegas under its Adult heading. A myriad of subheadings divide the Back Page adult world into escorts, body rubs, strippers and strip clubs, "dom & fetish" (domineering and fetish), "ts" (transsexual), male escorts, phone, and websites.

All of these web pages offer one a glimpse into the adult world of Las Vegas. There are <u>Female Escorts</u> for men and <u>Male Escorts</u> for women, and everything in between. For example, should a woman be looking for a <u>Male Russian Hunk</u>, he is available. A quick click on <u>his web page</u> will deliver the once-in-a-life-time-man-of-a-ladies-dreams. Who would have thought that this person would be found under male escorts on Back Page?

Massage Parlors and Spas

Massage parlors are ubiquitous to Las Vegas and the accepted practice of them providing *"happy endings"* is generally known. Las Vegas massage parlors range from the very fancy to the down right seedy, and from the upscale and legitimate to the spas that openly engage in prostitution. Most of the massage parlors and spas are found in strip malls in Las Vegas.

The establishments in the major hotels are generally referred to as health spas and unfortunately do not provide spa experiences like one would expect to receive in Asia. Probably the closest place that might meet this expectation is the Imperial Health Spa, a Korean spa that has very good reviews and is located on the North Side of Sahara Blvd across from the Commercial Center. The nudity, expected in this sort of establishment, invites the gay segment of the community, however the reviews indicate that patrons love the experience.

All massage and spa businesses in the Las Vegas area are legally licensed operations. They have business licenses posted in their lobby and municipal, city, or county codes apply to their operation. Many of these businesses have been around for years. A recent cutback in license issuances means that a new business cannot open up a parlor until another one goes out of business, or until one is closed by the city and a new slot for a license becomes available. Licenses are becoming more valuable and the services that are offered are becoming more competitive to attract higher paying customers.

Clark County has put some limits on new massage establishments to keep the number in control. The City of North Las Vegas and Henderson have limited the hours of the establishments so that they now must close by 10PM. However, the establishments have phone numbers and if one calls ahead, they may be accommodating after hours.

Massage parlors and spas wanting to continue to supply sexual services must continually work to circumvent the laws and codes that are written to prevent such activities. Operations that are forced to close are a result of complaints by neighboring businesses. In these cases, the leases are not renewed or the business is forced to close because of a sting operation that puts the owners in jail.

Rubmaps shows over 130 listings for Las Vegas. Henderson shows over 30. Some closures listed have moved to a new location in the city.

The basic income for massage therapists comes from tips that are given on top of the basic house price for a massage. That means that the masseuses are hungry to please, and will push the legal envelope to obtain a good tip. Tips usually run between $40 and $200 above the house price.

A reflexologist does not need to be licensed, but a massage therapist does. If the sign in front of an establishment shows "reflexology" and nothing else, it means the lady inside doesn't have a professional license for massage; thus, prices can be lower, on the order of $29 for a foot massage. Of course, services may likely migrate to a full massage or happy conclusion in the back room.

Some establishments are listed as Spas or Health Spas. These do not have to have licensed massage therapists and therefore do not fall under the codes written for massage parlors.

To skirt the laws and penalties, a number of establishments have hired their girls as independent contractors. Thusly, if the girls get into trouble for prostitution, they are the only ones that go to jail. Recently laws have been passed in the city of Henderson, NV to cause the "owner" of the massage business to suffer the same penalty as the person providing the service; therefore, if the massage therapist goes to jail, the owner goes to jail. This then eliminates the contractor relationship between owner and massage therapist, so to speak. The owner would then be subjected to the same $1,000 fine and 6 months in jail.

It is not clear how the penalties are adjudicated. It is possible that a lawyer gets the penalty changed to a lesser offense, the owner pays a fine, and business continues. Or perhaps the girls are now considered owners and the actual owners work at arms length. When a new law is written and on the books, the bad guys soon learn how to circumvent it. This is part of the changing life in Las Vegas.

All massage parlors have cameras in their lobby. These cameras serve several purposes. For one, they are used by the owners to determine how long a customer has been in the massage parlor, which establishes how much the house takes and how much the massage therapist owes the house. This pretty much keeps massage parlors operating on a clock basis.

In addition, the cameras can be used to identify undercover officers, so the girls will then know when a potential sting operation is coming down. The cameras can also be used to identify the idiots that come in to rob the establishment. Robbers have been known to come into a parlor and force a girl to provide services not agreed upon and then leave without paying. The massage parlor provides the police with photos, and in many cases license numbers of cars.

Finding Your Massage Parlor

Part of the fun of getting a massage is exploring and finding the right establishment with the right male or female practitioner, which can be as easy as getting into a cab and asking to be taken to a massage parlor! Online research is another possibility that can yield acceptable results. Here are some avenues to explore:

Rubmaps is one of the most complete erotic massage websites available. For a short while, access to the site is free and is usually long enough to check out a few massage parlors and to read older reviews. A one-month VIP membership costs $14.95 and provides VIP access to all the reviews. One can input their city and state, and a listing of all the local massage parlors will be given, along with reviews. Reviewers usually review the particular ladies at the establishment. This is a very entertaining and helpful site.

The site has a Slang-Tab that is helpful in understanding the sex menu and reviews. In some of the reviews, the slang such as FS (if underlined) will have a popup explanation. Example: FS (full service) = BJ + Sex. BJ = Blow Job. HJ = Hand Job. Pricing examples: Paid the House $70 for TS = Table Shower and got a HJ. Tip $60. Prices range from $50 to $200 for FS.

Erotic MP is a review site that requires payment upfront. A 30-day access sells for $24.95. This sort of website usually provides a bit more privacy for the establishments and the users. The police departments are less likely to be paying fees for their officers to have access.

Adult Search – Erotic Massage is a site that gives some reviews of massage parlors in Las Vegas. Reviews on this site are valuable to use for comparison to reviews on other sites. This is a free site with fewer reviews. In addition to massage parlors, adult search has other selections such as body rubs, which are out-call.

Naughty Reviews provides reasonable reviews of massage parlors. These are done well enough to compare with other reviews from different sites.

Massage Exchange at the Free Rub website is a brilliant social network for massage enthusiasts looking for massage partners with whom they can exchange massages. Registration is free. An upgrade allows messaging members to set up an exchange. No automatic repeat billing. The home page says that it is NOT an ADULT social network. However, if massage is your desire, this may be a way to set up a massage date for when you arrive in Las Vegas.

Vegas Spa Guide for Men is an on-line guide that provides some interesting reading. The blog provides reviews of nude spas for men. In general, "House Rules" suggest no interactions, but after reading a few reviews, one might conclude that there are exchanges being made when conditions are right. This site will alert new users to the "happenings" in the big Hotel Spas in Las Vegas.

Masseur Finder is a site for finding a masseur. The website indicates that the photographs are of the actual providers that are available for out-call or in-call. This site would most likely be good for males and females looking for a masseur.

Eros Guide to Massage Las Vegas is an all encompassing escort and massage (in-call and out-call service) site that has been available in Las Vegas for a number of years.

Street Hookers

One of the highest risk sexual encounters that you can pander to while in Las Vegas is the street hooker. Street hookers are monitored by undercover police in an effort to crack down on sex trafficking, especially of under aged girls. In addition, the hookers have pimps and other hookers maintaining a watchful eye. A young man recently arrested in Las Vegas for sex trafficking faces

Life Imprisonment. This is serious stuff; something a visitor to Las Vegas doesn't need to be, and shouldn't be, caught up in.

Customers that are enticed by street hookers can be fooled into tagging along with a lady into a side street or alleyway where they are commonly beat up and robbed. A quick look at the crime map will confirm the dangers of the streets of Las Vegas, especially during late night and early morning hours.

One may think that it is easy to go unnoticed with a hooker because the two might appear to "belong together." However, for the undercover police, it is relatively easy to see when two people don't belong together. The police, especially if they recognize the hooker, will walk up and ask a couple what they are up to and if they know each other. The couple may affirm that they indeed do know each other; however, when separated it becomes obvious that the two do not know each other's names or any other personal information. The mistake that men make is insisting that they are friends and that they just met.

One must remember that the girl may have been arrested numerous times prior to this encounter. See Working Girls for some real photos and how many times these girls have been arrested. In order to prevent matters from becoming insanely complex, out-of-control, and more incriminating, it is best to be honest and to work with the police. In most cases, the girl has been recognized by the police, will not have any ID, and will be arrested for loitering or disturbing the peace. The customer will be told to go on his way. This is where you can be a better consumer and divert your money and time to a more "accepted practice" in the city.

Hotels try to keep the "underage" or "bothersome" girls under control by using the hotel cameras. Hotel security gets used to seeing the same girls, gives them warnings, and eventually has them arrested for trespassing. They are then in serious trouble if they are caught on the premises again. However, the girls will most likely just move down the street to a new hotel. Some of these girls may be independent and work with hotel staff members; they tend to remain out of sight until they get a call from a bartender they know who just received a tip from a customer requesting a lady of the night.

The underage girls are the ones the police are trying to get off the street. They will prosecute both the "John" and the 'Hooker" in this case. As one police officer said, "It is so easy to take a drive to Pahrump and go to a brothel, or even to a massage parlor, than to get tangled up with an underage girl on the street." Be careful!

As a side note, the sex trafficking business is moving more toward the personals arena, which includes Backpage. If you are dealing direct with a person who has photos on a web page, then they are more established and you can at least see what you are getting. Outcall services that direct sex workers to your hotel room are a gamble because an under aged girl may arrive at your door. If in doubt, don't!

As a word of caution, become a better consumer and don't contribute to sex trafficking of underage girls. There are many good alternative options in Las Vegas. One can hire a legal aged escort, get a massage (escorts and massage), search (out-call or in-call services) through personals (be careful); or obtain a *"happy ending"* or more at an established massage parlor. Or, you can take a relaxing 80-minute drive to Pahrump and enjoy a great time getting exactly what you want at a legal brothel, discussed in Chapter 10.

> **Note:** *During the civil war, General Hooker of the Union army, in an attempt to protect his troops from VD, found the best ladies he could and pimped them to his men. The girls at that time were called Hooker's Girls. This is one of the earliest accounts of the term "hookers."*

TEN ITEMS TO REMEMBER ABOUT PROSTITUTION

1. "What happens in Las Vegas, stays in Las Vegas," is predominately true. If "What Happens" is breaking the law and dealing with the police, it will cost the tourist to make sure "It" "Stays in Las Vegas."

2. The Metro Police of Las Vegas and surrounding communities are focusing on sex trafficking of underage girls. This is serious stuff for a tourist to be caught up in and it is wise to avoid this area of prostitution.

3. What happens between consenting adults, 18 years of age or older, tends to be low on the Metro Police radar, mainly because of the difficulty in prosecution.

4. Periodic undercover stings in the sex industry keep participants (mainly providers) on the edge and in check. This includes bars and massage parlors.

5. Call girls, agency referrals, and street hookers are high-risk areas where the chances of being ripped off or arrested are increased.

6. The price range of full service sex ranges from $200 to over $1,000 an hour.

7. The most beautiful and experienced girls demand fees accordingly, and can be found at the more expensive hotels and VIP personals.

8. Massage parlors offer a broad range of services and are typically clean operations. Reviews of these establishments and those that provide services are easy to find. The massage therapists are required to be over 21, so it is less likely that they will be underage.

9. Most escorts, and those that offer sexual favors, in Las Vegas practice safe sex. Sexually transferrable diseases such as HIV and Lyme disease necessitate that one refrains from any bodily fluid transfer to prevent pathogen transfer. Play safe in Las Vegas!

10. It is very rare for a co-operative tourist to be busted along with a prostitute unless they are with underage girls. Co-operation with the police is the key to minimizing issues.

SWINGERS CLUBS

Swingers clubs are unique clubs that eliminate the hassle of cruising bars to find a fun evening with a like-minded consenting adult. At a swingers club, both people are there for the same reason and can be enjoying sex in less than 30 minutes. These clubs are straight forward, and most people feel comfortable with the group in a short period. The swingers clubs are very entertaining for an evening of fun, and with luck, one may score a once in a lifetime fantasy.

The <u>Las Vegas Red Rooster</u>, founded in 1982, is located in a private home that has grown to 13,000 square feet, is open 7 days a week, and hosts as many as 1,000 people a night. The owners, Chris and Mike, greet members every evening. Approximately 50% of the people there are regulars. If you are interested in meeting secure, down-to-earth people, this place is worth an evening of look-and-see entertainment.

The house is fashioned in a 1950's décor and has an indoor pool and a bar. It is a fascinating place to visit just to see who walks in the door and to watch people interact. You never know, you might be invited to a room for the experience of your life. The best time to go is after 10pm on Friday, Saturday, and Sunday. Visit the website for directions, FAQ's, The Rules, The Band, Photographs and more.

The Las Vegas Red Rooster is located to the east of Las Vegas at 6405 Greyhound Lane, Las Vegas, NV. The telephone number is 702-451-6661. Taxis have been known to long haul people to get higher fares so it is advised to use the taxis the club recommends on their directions page.

<u>The Fantasy Swingers Club</u> is another unique swingers club that is open 7 nights a week from 10pm to 4am. As stated on their website, Fantasy Swingers Club Las Vegas is the ultimate live sex show where consenting adult singles and couples play out their sexual fantasies and fetishes in a very intimate environment. They are located just off "The Strip" in the northeast corner of the Commercial Center at 953 E Sahara Ave, Ste B-17, in fabulous Las Vegas, Nevada, USA. The telephone number is 702-893-3977.

<u>Swingers Circle</u> is a unique swingers party that is open to small groups of people, typically 12 couples, and is famous on The Strip

as the "Orgy" party where everyone wants to get naked. The price is typically $80 per person. Phone number is 702-468-2774.

The Green Door is a well-known swingers club founded in 1998 in Las Vegas that provides a safe, clean environment for consenting adults. The club is not exactly in the best section of Las Vegas (The Commercial Center) so be careful after dark as there are many prostitutes cruising around. In a recent Green Door Yelp review it was suggested that couples bring their own blanket, alcohol wipes and something to sit on when naked. There are many cabs outside so this place is easy in and easy out. The reviews are mixed and should be read before going.

Finding like-minded swingers is relatively easy in Las Vegas. A straightforward web operation to locate swingers in Las Vegas is sdc.com. Registration is required.

GAY ACTIVITIES

Las Vegas is full of gay activities, as noted in Chapter 6 - Gay Clubs and Bars, and many are centered in the Gay Quarter and the Commercial Center. Off the beaten track is the BlueMoon Hotel, a male only, clothing optional gay resort designed to meet the needs of the gay male. BlueMoon Yelp reviews are mixed.

When browsing some of the better-known gay websites for Las Vegas, there is nothing left to the imagination. Gay activities are a big part of the city and will most likely be expanding.

Rentboy is a male escort, gay massage, and gay male escort service.

Men4rentnow is a gay male and gay massage service that lists over 50 well-endowed men that are available for escort or massage services.

Rentmen is a gay male service that lists approximately 29 men available in Las Vegas. This website does not require registration and provides easy contact with service providers.

Squirt is a gay cruising website that gives information on where gays go and what they are looking for based on location.

Hawks Gym is advertised as a gay owned and operated men's club that provides the gay and bisexual men of the community with a safe, sane, and healthy environment. It is located in the Commercial Center District, and is a discrete place to meet gay men and share similar experiences. The facility has been well received and is active in the local gay community.

Entourage Vegas Spa & Health Club, located in the Commercial Center District, is a gay health spa. The website also provides extensive listings of gay activities in Las Vegas including the gay bars.

The Imperial Health Spa, a Korean spa that operates as one might expect in Asia, and is the only one of its kind in the city. For a taste of the orient, this just might be a satisfying experience. Imperial Health Spa Services are extensive; the place gets good reviews, and the prices are reasonable especially with Groupon Spa Pass where you can save up to 50%. It is located across the street from the Commercial Center District.

Smart phone apps, Appendix G, can be narrowed down to lifestyle where one can find gays with like interests that are nearby.

10
LEGAL PROSTITUTION – BROTHELS

Nevada is the only state in the United States where <u>prostitution is legal</u> in regulated brothels. Prostitution is practiced in eight of Nevada's sixteen counties. It is illegal in counties with populations over 700,000, which includes Clark County and the city of Las Vegas, and Washoe County and the city of Reno.

Even though <u>prostitution</u> in Las Vegas is illegal, it is of common practice. However, if one wants to remain *"legal"* without taking a chance on making a mistake, then a *"legal"* brothel may be the wisest of decisions.

The closest brothels to Las Vegas are in Pahrump, 80 miles to the Southwest in Nye County. Most of the brothels in Nevada are located in and around Reno, NV. The minimum age to enter a Brothel in Nye County is 21. Most brothels have a bar on site.

To get to a Pahrump brothel from Las Vegas, a taxi ride will cost $250 round trip and includes wait time. The taxi will call ahead and the house will pay the driver 20 to 30% of what the customer pays the brothel. The house and prostitute typically split the negotiated price for services, but the taxi fare typically comes out of the prostitute's share.

Some brothels offer free round-trip limousine service from Las Vegas. The limousine fare also comes out of what the customer pays the brothel. If a limousine is chartered for the ride to Pahrump, the client typically pays the limousine fee; the limousine will call ahead to the brothel and will still receive a portion of what the client spends at the brothel. Expect the minimum fee at the brothel to be rather steep. The client is expected to be handing over at least $1,000.

The best way to put the most money into a prostitute's pocket and to get the best-bang-for-your-buck is to drive a private vehicle to Pahrump. The one-hour trip is beautiful, especially in the early morning or late afternoon, and the roads are excellent. Even if one is not interested in taking part in the activities offered, it makes for an interesting few hours to have a drink, talk to the ladies, and to enjoy the free tours to see how the places operate.

There are approximately 28 operating brothels in Nevada. The two brothels in Pahrump closest to Las Vegas are Sheri's Ranch and Chicken Ranch. Both operate in a similar fashion and are right next door to each other.

Sheri's Ranch is the more expensive, high-end brothel near Las Vegas. It is actually a hotel. A prostitute with good ratings will cost upwards of $1,000 per hour. Upon entering the establishment and walking into the bar area, one will see a number of the ladies at tables; usually there are up to 20 ladies resident at any one time. A coordinator greets incoming patrons.

Prior to visiting Sheri's Ranch, a quick on-line review of the lineup is well worth the time if you want to know about the ladies that will be there. The ladies can also be contacted by email to arrange for a meeting time. Let the coordinator know which lady is of interest and ask for a tour. The lady of choice will show and explain the sex menu and tell a little about the themed bungalow suites. The tour also includes viewing the different rooms that are available and gives some of the inside information about what goes on there.

At this point, if one is interested in spending time with the lady, they will be guided to her room where the negotiation for price and activities takes place. Depending on the lady, prices are in the $10,000 range for the complete menu. The negotiations are monitored.

Many of the ladies at Sheri's Ranch reside in Los Angeles and San Francisco. Some are actresses and models that supplement their incomes with short tours at the brothel. Here is an example of a hi-end lady; a beautiful professional model that speaks multiple languages, has an interesting accent, and is fun to talk with. All the ladies at these brothels undergo regular medical checkups. The ladies do appreciate men with good hygiene.

Sheri's Ranch is well worth the visit even if one is not going to indulge in the activities; it is located at 10413 Homestead Rd, Pahrump, NV, (775) 727-591.

And right next door is the Chicken Ranch.

The Chicken Ranch is another enticing brothel that offers beautiful ladies such as this petite young hottie. This brothel has a colorful history originating in Texas. The process of selecting a lady is similar to Sheri's Ranch. Ladies can be communicated with via email. A patron will negotiate with the ladies in private by discussing the desired activities and amount of money available. At this point, time and service will be discussed. The house generally monitors the negotiation so that they know the lady is not cheating on funds. Money is transferred to the house prior to the clock starting.

Specialty parties and couples are also welcome and there are ladies at the brothel that will accommodate most activities. The Chicken Ranch is located at 10511 Homestead Rd, Pahrump, NV, (775) 727-5721.

The other brothels are more distant from Las Vegas.

Shady Lady Ranch (Scotty's Junction, NV) Located on Highway 95 south of Scotty's Junction between Mile Markers 91 and 92 on US95, 31 miles North of Beatty, Nevada. Call 1-866-301-5855 or 775-321-3126.

Love Ranch Southern NV - Crystal, Nevada. Love Ranch is located 5 miles south on Highway 160 from the junction of US 95 North and Hwy 160. Call (775) 372-5251.

11
DRUGS

The drug scene in the United States has been uprooted and distorted since the 1960's when smoking weed was the thing to do and few people knew what cocaine and heroin were; now it affects every part of our society in ways that one would never have imagined. The high drug usage today, coupled with the war on drugs puts the U.S. in the lead for incarcerating more citizens per capita than any country in the world. The privatization of incarceration facilities only contributes to the money being made off this industry, and is thought to be a big factor in the increased incarceration rate.

In Las Vegas, an interesting indicator of where drug use can be seen is in the local high schools. A quick informal survey of high school students indicates that virtually 100% of them use drugs, from smoking weed to using cocaine and heroin. It is no wonder that Las Vegas crime rates are so high. Perhaps the availability of drugs for high school students is an offshoot of the massive availability of drugs in the city of Las Vegas.

The demand for drugs in this city is incredible, as one drug dealer recently interviewed on a television documentary indicated, "Sixty percent of people coming to Las Vegas come here for drugs." If one were to couple illegal drug usage with the overuse of prescription drugs, and even the purported issue of doctors giving prescriptions to tourists, one might assume that Las Vegas has the largest drug usage rate of any city in the world.

While we don't know if Vegas ranks number one, we do know that Nevada has the distinction of being the 4th ranked state for prescription drug overdose deaths. Perhaps the distinction of Las Vegas ranking second in the United States in 2004 for illegal drug use was a telling trend for the country as a whole. If the estimate of 46,052 combined drug users in Las Vegas is accurate, then the city has an abuse rate of 5.78%, a number that is truly staggering.

When drugs are sold without interruption in front of a Las Vegas Wal-Mart, it is obvious that there is a problem. As early as 2007, the Metro Police indicated methamphetamine use at epidemic proportions. At that time, illegal drugs were found to be coming into Las Vegas at an alarming rate, and today most would agree they are still flowing into the city unabated.

With the huge population trend (under stats and facts) increasing from roughly 273,000 in 1970 to over 2.06 million in 2013, one can start appreciating the problem. Couple these numbers with the estimated 22 million illegal drug and 131 million alcohol users in the United States and the "What happens in Las Vegas, Stays in Las Vegas" reputation, and one can easily see the huge demand for all sorts of drugs in the city.

Drugs in Las Vegas are easy to obtain. A quick search on the web produced an interesting article on How to Score Weed in Las Vegas. A cocktail waitress indicated that at one club drugs were provided to customers and employees. Price of Weed is website that provides current prices for Marijuana in Las Vegas and other Nevada cities.

The Las Vegas gentlemen's clubs and nightclubs are the party places where much drug usage occurs. Ecstasy, cocaine, methamphetamine, GHB, and heroin are common in the clubs and are the main drugs involved in arrests in Las Vegas.

When visiting Las Vegas, if one is inclined to use drugs, then it is perhaps wise to at least know of a local attorney who defends tourists in drug related crimes. Appendix F has a complete list of attorneys, phone numbers, web links, and other valuable information.

A former prosecutor's website provides valuable information on Las Vegas drug laws and penalties, and presents some good advice on different defenses used. This information is something any drug user should be aware of, as what is said and done at the time of an arrest can make a big difference in a defense. What is also interesting is that even with a serious drug arrest, a client may be able to be fully defended while out of state, keeping the process confidential. Like traffic tickets, serious offenses may be reduced (if one is lucky) to the equivalent of a parking ticket or a steep fine, plus attorney's fees.

The gangs in Las Vegas are the biggest drug sellers. What the Metro Police try to do is keep the drugs that are cut with poisonous materials off the street, or, at least, put a dent in their availability. They will go undercover and nail sellers on the street.

Drugs sell for twice as much on The Strip as they do off beat. But if you go off the track, you are opening yourself up to be robbed. It is important to know that for gang dealers, it is just as easy to steal your money and save the drugs for another sale; so getting ripped off is a big issue.

One should be extremely careful in Vegas when looking for drugs.

THE UNDERGROUND FDA

The best website for learning about drugs in Las Vegas is <u>Dance Safe,</u> one of the most comprehensive websites on drugs available. If one is using drugs, they should be intimately aware of this site and the information therein. The Las Vegas Metro Police refer to this site themselves to know what is going in the illegal drug industry.

An example of reporting on their website:

"According to federal officials observing drug trends and monitoring public-health problems, drug traffickers have adulterated much of the cocaine in the United States with a substance called levamisole, mostly used to de-worm livestock but also used in humans as part of certain cancer treatments."

There is a <u>Dance Safe Test Kit</u> to help users evaluate some of the drugs. This web page describes how to use the kit and how different drugs show up when tested. Dance Safe periodically has excellent articles for those that are using different drugs on how to be safe. Nothing like becoming an informed user and taking responsibility for what one is doing.

The <u>Drug Aid</u> European website has some good information on safe practices to reduce many of the risks associated with drug use.

The <u>Detox Answers</u> website offers answers to many questions about drugs that one may never think of asking.

Heard about <u>Moon Rocks: The Best High On Earth</u>? Well it is MDMA (Ecstasy) and it may be cut with some nasty stuff. This *LA Weekly* article gets straight to the point and is worth a read. The comments from some of MDMA users at the end of the article are priceless. <u>Ecstasydata.org</u> collects, reviews, manages, and publishes laboratory pill testing results from a variety of organizations.

Be safe!

12
GUNS

Many people come to Las Vegas from places like California, Illinois, Canada, Australia, and cities such as Chicago and Washington, D.C. to shoot all sorts of guns that are insanely illegal back home. They take pictures to show friends that they too can be Rambo and can shoot 50 cal. machine guns, holster a Desert Eagle, pocket a Judge, or handle a real AK-47.

Nevada gun laws are some of the most liberal in the country. Local residents can own machine guns and even real James Bond silencers for handguns. This is one very cool state when it comes to the possession of firearms. Clark County reports that over 45% of households own guns. It is believed that the average household in Henderson, NV, one of the safest cities in the United States, has 6 guns.

In case you fear for your life when coming to Las Vegas, here is something to ponder: In Las Vegas, where guns are legal, the murder and non-negligent manslaughter rate is 7.6 per 100,000 people. This compares to 15.2, the rate for the City of Chicago, where up until a recent Supreme Court Ruling, guns were illegal. Until recently, if you were found with a handgun in your possession in Chicago, you went to jail for two to five years and were fined $25,000. Not so in Nevada. This difference is important, as it is a result of the <u>Tenth Amendment to the Constitution</u>, which refers to States' Rights in the USA.

CONCEALED CARRY

The State of Nevada has <u>Concealed Firearms Permits</u> for residents and non-residents that pass the test and the background check.

The Nevada Concealed Carry website provides all the required information for obtaining permits. Many local residents carry concealed firearms.

To carry a concealed firearm, one needs a CCW (Carry Concealed Weapon) permit. You do not have to live in Nevada to be eligible for a Nevada CCW Permit. If you have an out-of-state CCW permit, check the Nevada Department of Public Safety web page to see if your states' permits are recognized in the State of Nevada.

FIREARMS TRAINING

For those interested in firearms training, 5 Arrows Tactical Training, and Las Vegas Firearms Training offer training classes as well as CCW permit classes. For more in-depth training, Front Sight Firearms Training Institute is located in Pahrump.

DESERT SHOOTING

Guns can be taken out on Bureau of Land Management property and shot "*where permitted.*" Maps and current information can be picked up at the BLM Southern Nevada District Office located at 4701 North Torrey Pines, Las Vegas, Nevada 89130. Phone Number: 702-515-5000 and Office Hours: 7:30 a.m. - 4:30 p.m., M-F.

BLM lands are hard to identify, as can be seen on the Las Vegas Interactive Map. Go under the Administrative Boundaries tab, and check BLM Lands. This map will then have to be crossed checked with closure maps. Since there are generally no signs that differentiate lands, finding a shooting area on BLM land that is currently open becomes a formidable task.

Refer to the Las Vegas Valley Target Shooting Closure Map for information on closed areas. This is a slow loading PDF document.

Refer to the Pahrump Closure Map for closed areas near Pahrump.

FIREARM SHIPMENT

If you are from out-of-state, you can bring your own gun. You can ship them directly to Las Vegas to save yourself the hassle of taking them on an airplane or in your car. Call Paul Davidson of Davidson's Firearms located just south of the I215 freeway on Eastern. This is very close to McCarran International Airport. They will hold your gun for pickup and will send it back to your FFL for pickup.

> Davidson's Firearms
> 108 S. Eastern Ave. Ste 103
> Henderson, NV 89052
> 702-456-6600

SHOOTING RANGES IN LAS VEGAS

The Range 702 is an indoor range, one of the largest west of the Mississippi, and the largest in Las Vegas. It has 25 lanes and a nice café where you can relax while watching your friends through glass windows. PRISM interactive video simulators are set up for four of the lanes and cost $25 for 50 shots. PRISM provides simulated real life "shoot or not to shoot" decisions using a real gun. This is an outstanding exercise to help one think before acting.

The Range 702 offers a full range of guns for rent including machine guns, rifles, pistols, and shotguns. In addition to safety classes, The Range 702 offers concealed carry permit courses and women's self-defense classes. The range is located just west of the Strip. A good experience here will cost you $200 and will last several hours. There is a VIP lounge.

> The Range 702
> 4699 Dean Martin Dr.
> Las Vegas, Nevada 89103
> 702-485-3232

Range fees range from $50 – $200 for 30 min to 2 hours. Range time $10/hr.

Limousine pickup is available.

The Gun Store, also located near the Strip, though smaller than The Range 702, has some pretty sharp looking young ladies and some good looking dudes to help you out with a good selection of guns to shoot.

> The Gun Store
> 2900 E. Tropicana Ave.
> Las Vegas, Nevada
> 702-454-1110

Machine Guns Vegas has expanded their experience to include outdoor activities; one is a helicopter ride to the Pro Gun Range in Henderson near Boulder City. Should you want to learn why the USA Military costs so much money to operate, it might be worth shooting the electric rotary driven 8-Barrel Mini-Gatling gun. This sucker shoots more bullets than one can count. Take your camera.

> Machine Guns Vegas
> 3501 Aldebaran Ave.
> Las Vegas, Nevada 89102
> 1-800-757-4668

A well-regarded experience is Battlefield Vegas where one can engage in firing most new and old military weapons. This gun shooting activity rates very high on Trip Advisor. Battlefield Vegas even has an offsite location outside of Las Vegas for some real exciting fun.

> Battlefield Vegas
> 2771 Industrial Road
> Las Vegas, Nevada 89109
> 1-702-566-1000

OUTDOOR RANGES

Pro Gun Club is an ever-expanding gun club that offers an excellent outdoor shooting experience. They work with the Sure Fire Institute that offers many gun-training courses. At Pro Gun Club, they offer a Blow-Sh!t-Up opportunity where you can shoot some amazing stuff at old cars. This is definitely an E-ticket gun experience.

Don't be afraid to take a 30-minute ride out toward Boulder City for a stop at the Pro Gun Club, especially if you want to take in the Hoover Dam or the Big Bridge. Admission to the range is $20 for out of state residents. The place has <u>great reviews</u>.

<u>Pro Gun Club</u>
12801 S. US 95 Hwy
Boulder City, Nevada 89005
702-293-2108

Hours are 7am to 5pm

The <u>Clark County Shooting Complex</u> is one of the largest and most modern shooting ranges in the United States. It does not advertise because it is a Clark County facility, so the complex is underused and not crowded. The facilities include an archery center, shotgun (trap and skeet), rifle-pistol (25, 50, 100 and 200 yards), an education center for training, and the complex even has an RV site.

The CCSC is located at the extreme north end of the Las Vegas metropolitan area, approximately 20 minutes from the Strip. This is an easy to use facility with reasonable prices. In the time it would take to find a place in the desert, you can be shooting from nice concrete gun benches. Also, you will not have to worry about safety issues from indiscriminate desert shooters. Here is an excellent <u>Clark County Shooting Complex review.</u>

<u>Clark County Shooting Complex</u>
11357 North Decatur Boulevard
Las Vegas, Nevada 89131
(702) 455-2000

13

PREFERRED CARDS, BUFFETS, AND RESTAURANTS

There are many ways to find quality and to save money in Las Vegas. Many people shop around for hotel rooms and packages before visiting; however, upon arrival they may pay premium prices for food, movies, and other services that are offered at discount prices for Preferred Card members. They may go to the buffet in the local or nearby hotel when much better and lower priced buffets are offered elsewhere. In Las Vegas, specials, preferred cards, and reviews are an excellent way to approach the overwhelming city of choices.

PREFERRED CARDS

Even if going to a hotel just for a buffet, it is recommended that you sign-up for a preferred card; it is as easy as showing your driver's license. The card may provide an immediate discount for buffets and movies. Many places offer senior discounts on top of preferred card discounts. A good practice upon entering any hotel in Las Vegas is to sign-up for their preferred card.

Use your mobile device to look up reviews. One of the best review sites for Las Vegas is YELP. It is always good to look at current reviews to evaluate the status of a business. In addition, it is always advisable to keep an eye open for 2-for-1 coupons at Coupon Grabber. Also, Tix4tonight offers 25% to 50% discounts on the day of offering or the next day.

BUFFETS

One may become overwhelmed with information on buffets when arriving in Las Vegas. Many hotels offer buffets and provide a discount for hotel guests that have registered for their preferred card. From then on, it is up to you to ask around and do your own research. Here are a few articles to help you get started.

Trip Advisor has a good article on the <u>Best Buffets in Las Vegas</u> where one can opt for the Buffet-of-Buffet Wrist Band. The website 10best.com also has an article, <u>Ten Las Vegas Buffets That Take All You Can Eat To A New Level</u>.

Downsizing that number a little is a USA Today Travel article <u>Vegas buffets: five to find</u>. In addition, Travel Channel Buffets Las Vegas does their write-up on <u>Best Buffets in Las Vegas</u>.

The ins-and-outs of a <u>24 Hour Buffet Pass</u> are discussed at the Top Buffet website. This excellent article may save a bit of time and frustration and is a necessary read if one is considering a 24-hour buffet pass. At ezinearticles.com, <u>Jules Monty</u> writes a good review on the same topic.

The 2 for 1 coupon and the $5 off coupons are still regarded as the best way to go for overall savings without over eating; however, Top Buffet provides some up to the minute special buffet deals offered at different hotels for good savings.

Buffets in Las Vegas are serious activities for those that are interested in quality food and want lots of it. To miss the long lines, getting there at opening time (around 5:30) reduces the sore legs. Be prepared for up to 2-hour waits on holidays and at prime dinner times between 6 and 9 PM. There is nothing wrong with going for the $10.99 breakfast buffet in the morning and staying a little late for the changeover to the lunch buffet to add a little variety to the menu.

The <u>Feast Buffet</u>, located on the gaming level of the <u>Green Valley Ranch Resort</u>, is a nicely priced buffet with a reasonably good selection of food. Prices range from $6.99 for breakfast to $13.00 with a **Station Casino's Boarding Pass** discount card. The card is easy to register for on your way in from the top level of the parking garage. The Boarding Pass is good at any of the Station Casinos, The Red Rock Casino Resort and Spa, Green Valley Ranch Resort, and the Fiesta Hotel.

> Green Valley Ranch Resort
> 2300 Paseo Verde Parkway
> Henderson, Nevada 89052
> (702) 617-7777, Toll Free: (866) 782-9487

The Festival Buffet, at the Fiesta Hotel in Henderson, is a nice place to try the $0.99 breakfast buffet in the morning on your way out to Hoover Dam, The Bridge, or an early day of shooting at the Pro Gun Club.

> Fiesta Hotel in Henderson
> 777 W. Lake Mead Pkwy
> Henderson, Nevada 89015
> (702) 558-7000, Toll Free: (888) 899-7770

The Studio B Buffet, located on the casino level at the M Resort Spa Casino, offers one of the best Seafood Buffets in Las Vegas at $39.99 on the weekends and holidays. Standard Buffets are $23.99 during the week. The Breakfast Buffet is $10.99.

> M Resort Spa Casino
> 12300 Las Vegas Blvd S.
> Henderson, Nevada 89044
> (702) 797-1000

The Village Seafood Buffet at the Rio Las Vegas is truly spectacular, offering "all-seafood, all-the-time, all-you-can-eat." The buffet features lobster, snow crab legs, shrimp, freshly shucked oysters, sushi, and much more. The trip around the world Village Seafood Buffet offers a unique variety of flavors representing the Mediterranean, the Pacific Rim, the Baja region, South America, and North America. This buffet is well worth the visit.

> Rio Las Vegas
> *3700 W. Flamingo Road*
> *Las Vegas, Nevada 89103*
> *(866) 746-7671*

The Bistro Buffet at the Palms Casino Resort is described by Top Buffet as the Best Cheap Buffet in Vegas.

> The Palms Casino Resort
> 4321 West Flamingo Road
> Las Vegas, Nevada 89103
> (866) 942-7770

The Buffet at the Wynn is regarded as one of the better buffets in the city and is well worth the time and money. This is an elegant restaurant with a beautiful setting.

> Wynn Las Vegas and Encore Hotel
> 3131 Las Vegas Blvd. South
> Las Vegas, Nevada 89109
> (702) 770-7000, Toll Free: (888) 320-7123

Remember the **Station Casino's Boarding Pass** is good at Fiesta, Station Casinos, Green Valley Ranch, and Wildfire casinos. Preferred cards get you some great discounts!

EXCELLENT RESTAURANTS

Las Vegas is filled with restaurants and they have to be good to stay in business, which means they must offer value, quality, and good service. When any of these attributes slip, the restaurant is almost guaranteed to go under. The customer reviews don't provide any slack and the competition is stiff in Las Vegas. Restaurants that survive for a few years are generally good stand-ins for a nice meal. Trip Advisor ranks over 3,000 restaurants in Las Vegas, and is worth a look to see which restaurants are in the top 20 of the list.

A good rule of thumb for dining out in Las Vegas is to check the reviews before going. Yelp reviews are the best for getting the latest run down on eating establishments. Also, you can get a voucher from Tix4Tonight for some restaurants and save as much as 25% on food and alcohol. Here are a few "no miss" establishments:

Basking in 115 years of family history, an evening at RAO's Las Vegas will be an unforgettable dining experience. Known for its "perfectly cooked pastas, risottos and mouthwatering steak bistecca" this restaurant will not disappoint. This award-winning Italian Restaurant is well known for serving the best meatballs in Las Vegas. See RAO's reviews on Yelp.

>RAO's Las Vegas
>Caesars Palace Las Vegas Hotel & Casino
>3570 Las Vegas Boulevard South
>Las Vegas, Nevada 89109
>(702) 731-7267

Located downtown on Fremont Street, Hugo's Cellar is the romantic spot to take your sweetheart in Las Vegas. A beautiful rose will be presented to the lady upon seating, which sets the pace for a fine, unforgettable dining experience. If there was only one choice to pick for a "can't miss" evening, Hugo's Cellar is the place. Reservations are recommended. Take a limo to top it off. See Hugo's Reviews on Yelp. Afterwards, walk out in front of the Four Queens and enjoy the Fremont Experience.

>Hugo's Cellar *at the*
>Four Queens Hotel and Casino
>202 Fremont St
>Las Vegas, Nevada 89101
>(702) 385-4011

Located in the MGM Grand, Tom Colicchio's Craftsteak is a good steak house that is easily accessible along the Strip in the MGM Grand Hotel. See Tom Colicchio's reviews on Yelp.

>Tom Colicchio's Craftsteak
>3799 Las Vegas Boulevard S
>Las Vegas, Nevada 89109
>(702) 891-7318

North of East Flamingo Road, Del Frisco's Double Eagle Steak House is a good alternative, high review steak house. See Del Frisco's reviews on Yelp.

>Del Frisco's Double Eagle Steak House
>3925 Paradise Rd
>Las Vegas, Nevada 89169
>(702) 796-0063

Located in the Paris Hotel, The Eiffel Tower Restaurant has an incredible view and fabulous French food. The menu is broad and has a great selection to meet most anyone's appetite. See the Eiffel Tower Restaurant reviews on Yelp.

> Eiffel Tower Restaurant
> 3655 Las Vegas Blvd S.
> Las Vegas, Nevada 89109
> (702) 948-6937

Lawry's The Prime Rib Steakhouse is a high end, excellent steak house that specializes in Prime Rib. It continually gets high reviews, is well known, and has high standards. See Lawry's The Prime Rib Steakhouse reviews on Yelp.

> Lawry's The Prime Rib
> 4043 Howard Hughes Pkwy
> Las Vegas, Nevada 89169
> Neighborhood: Eastside
> (702) 893-2223

Located in the South Las Vegas suburb area, the new Soho Japanese Restaurant has been getting some great reviews, and is well worth the visit for a surprise dining experience. Every dish is high quality and the prices are right; it is an all around high value restaurant. See Soho Japanese Restaurant reviews on Yelp.

> Soho Japanese Restaurant
> 7377 S. Jones Blvd.
> Las Vegas, Nevada 89139
> (702) 776-7778

Located in the Henderson Executive Airport, The Landings HND Restaurant is an excellent, quiet location for a quaint breakfast or lunch. You will most likely meet the owner Marie, and she will make sure your experience is enjoyable. The small restaurant, sitting above the terminal building with a great view of the runway and private jet ramp, can be overloaded on holidays and special occasions so call ahead. Reservations are not needed. Parking is simple at the small airport parking lot and the restaurant is a short walk inside the terminal. See The Landings HND Restaurant reviews on Yelp and Trip Advisor.

> The Landings HND Restaurant
> 3500 Executive Terminal Drive
> Henderson, Nevada 89052
> 702-616-3337

Top of the World Restaurant, located on the top of the Stratosphere, has one of the best views in Las Vegas. The restaurant does a complete rotation in one hour and is recommended because of its photograph opportunities. Try to get your reservation table so that you will be facing WEST during the Nocturnal Dusk and Astronomical Dusk periods when the sky is a wonderful dark blue and the lights can be seen in a photograph. If you ask to be seated on the north side of the restaurant at the beginning of Nocturnal Dusk, you will be facing south, at approximately the end of Astronomical Dusk looking straight down the Strip. Check Chapter 16 – Photography for the free smart phone apps to help you determine this period. See the Top of the World reviews on Yelp before you go. Vegas.com has a good written review and periodic discount offers.

> Top of the World Stratosphere
> Stratosphere Casino, Hotel & Tower
> 2000 Las Vegas Boulevard
> Las Vegas, Nevada 89104
> 702-380-7711

Lotus of Siam is a renowned Thai restaurant located on Sahara Ave. just east of Las Vegas Blvd in the Commercial Center District of Las Vegas. Chef Saipin Chutima has an incredible knack in the kitchen that has taken this tiny place to top listings in North America. The food is excellent and worth any wait. The news articles on the walls, and the signed photos of famous people, are exciting to look over. The wine list is beyond incredible. It is suggested that you arrive for an early supper as the tiny place gets packed during dinner hours. Lotus of Siam is rated #9 of 3,797 restaurants in Las Vegas on Trip Advisor. Lotus of Siam also has good reviews on Yelp.

Lotus of Siam
953 E. Sahara Ave, Suite A5
Las Vegas, NV 89104
702-735-3030

There are also some of those irresistible-eating places that specialize in pizza and burgers. Look at Best Pizza in Las Vegas and Best Burgers in Las Vegas for the top 10 of each. From the Best Burgers in Las Vegas, don't miss out Bachi Burgers.

14
ENTERTAINMENT

L ocals will tell you that the Cirque shows are the best entertainment for the money in Las Vegas. Millions of dollars have been spent on the permanent stages and props for the eight Cirque du Soleil shows, so they will be around for a while in order to recoup investment. These shows are excellent, have great reviews, and are worth the money.

If you are going to Las Vegas to see a few shows, the Cirque du Soleil should be on the top of your list. There are many to choose from including **LOVE - The Beatles** at the Mirage, **Zumanity** at New York, **Mystère** at Treasure Island, **Criss Angel Believe** at the Luxor, **O** at the Bellagio, **KÀ** at the MGM Grand, **Zarkana** at Aria Resort & Casino, and **Michael Jackson ONE** at the Mandalay.

Tix4tonight may be offering some good discount tickets (up to 50%) for the Cirque shows; these are usually for sale only for same day shows. It is good to either call for details or to go to Tix4tonight for locations. The Tix4tonight location map shows all the booth locations.

Best of Vegas also has some good deals worth checking. The SmarterVegas website is another place to look for good ticket offerings. If you start with the Cirque shows, it is much easier to narrow down a particular show to meet your entertainment calendar.

Vegas.com has each show listed with ticket prices and a "More Info" link that provides a good review of each show. Additionally, Show tickets.com will provide some current opportunities.

CIRQUE DU SOLEIL SHOWS

Cirque du Soleil -- Love – The Beatles at the Mirage Las Vegas is a beautifully well-choreographed show of dance and acrobatics to the sounds of the Beatles. There are 6,341 speakers surrounding the audience and every seat is less than 100 feet from the center stage, which is redefined on the fly. This is a "can't miss" show that is guaranteed to be a pleaser. Visit Vegas.com for a detailed review and tickets.

Cirque du Soleil -- Zumanity at the New York New York – Las Vegas Hotel & Casino is an uninhibited sexually biased show with some incredible acrobatics and audience interaction. This show will please anyone who is tempted to explore the many sides of sexuality. Visit Vegas.com for a detailed review and tickets.

Cirque du Soleil -- Mystère at the Treasure Island Hotel and Casino - Las Vegas may be thought of as an acrobatic show that is carried to the extreme so that at every turn you are marveling about how it was done. Mystère is a funny, entertaining show that is worth seeing. Visit Vegas.com for a detailed review and tickets.

Cirque du Soleil -- Criss Angel Believe at the Luxor Las Vegas is a magic act that is filled with suspense and wonder. It is a praiseworthy act with outstanding props, assistants, and it is filled with drama and illusion. This is a Cirque show you either like or don't like. Visit Vegas.com for a detailed review and tickets.

Cirque du Soleil -- O at the Bellagio – Las Vegas is an aquatic act that has to be witnessed. The show includes a million gallon pool, a score of acrobats and synchronized swimmers, and nearly a hundred performers who appear and disappear underwater. The stage, which switches from pool to dry terra firma in seconds, is only part of the incredible nature of this show. Visit Vegas.com for a detailed review and tickets.

Cirque du Soleil -- KÀ at the MGM Grand is a story with a plot that is told on a $200 million stage. This show should be rated high on the list to see while visiting Las Vegas. Visit Vegas.com for a detailed review and tickets.

Cirque du Soleil -- <u>Zarkana</u> at the <u>Aria Resort & Casino</u> will take you on a strange and mystifying journey though a world that only a Cirque show can create. From snakes to spiders, the Zarkana performers are a "well orchestrated" and talented group guaranteed to provide a memorable Las Vegas experience. Visit <u>Vegas.com</u> for a detailed review and tickets.

Cirque du Soleil -- <u>Michael Jackson ONE</u> at the <u>Mandalay Bay</u> is a tribute to the legendary performer. Four different characters receive items from Michael's past and go on to demonstrate the incredible allure of his different talents. This is a-must-see Cirque show for Michael Jackson fans. Visit <u>Vegas.com</u> for a detailed review and tickets.

ENTERTAINMENT SHOWS

There are many shows in Las Vegas, more to see than there is time for, even with many visits. You can select one at a whim, via a free or reduced fare ticket, or by an invite from friends. Some advance planning can save a lot of money. <u>Show tickets.com</u> is a good place to start. The front web page shows some of the current running shows.

ADULT SHOWS

Showtickets.com has a complete current listing of <u>Adult Shows</u> with current ticket prices.

<u>Thunder Down Under</u> at the <u>Excalibur Hotel Casino</u>

<u>Chippendales</u> at the <u>Rio Las Vegas</u>

<u>Absinthe</u> at <u>Caesars Palace Las Vegas</u>

<u>Jubilee</u> at <u>Bally's Casino Las Vegas</u>

<u>X Rocks</u> at the <u>Rio Las Vegas</u>

<u>X Burlesque</u> at the <u>Flamingo Las Vegas</u>

<u>Night School 4 Girls</u> at the <u>Hard Rock Café Las Vegas</u>

<u>Pin Up</u> at the <u>Stratosphere</u>

BROADWAY/THEATER

Showtickets.com has complete listing of Broadway/Theater shows with current ticket prices.

> Rock of Ages at the Venetian
>
> Blue Man Group at the Monte Carlo Las Vegas Resort and Casino
>
> Le Rêve (The Dream and the Back Stage Tour) at the Wynn Resort and Casino
>
> Jersey Boys at the Paris Las Vegas Hotel and Casino
>
> Dancing Queen at Planet Hollywood Resort
>
> Vegas the Show at Planet Hollywood Resort
>
> Jabbawockeez at the Monte Carlo Las Vegas Resort and Casino
>
> Menopause the Musical at the Luxor Las Vegas
>
> Million Dollar Quartet at Harrah's Las Vegas

MAGIC/HYPNOSIS

There are a number of magic and hypnosis shows in Las Vegas, but none compare to the well-known act of David Copperfield.

> David Copperfield at the MGM Grand

WELL-KNOWN STARS

Do a Google search on your favorite stars and see if they have shows scheduled for Las Vegas. You might just strike it lucky!

A number of entertainers are scheduled at Caesars Palace including Jerry Seinfeld, Shania Twain, Rod Stewart, Celine Dion, and Elton John.

At the Mirage Las Vegas you can you can enjoy the talents of Jay Leno and other Aces of Comedy.

Rodney Carrington is at the MGM Grand Hotel. Check the MGM Grand Entertainment Calendar to see some of the big names that might be scheduled in the future.

15
ADRENALINE RUSH

If you're looking for an extreme adrenaline rush, then "DO" the Adrenaline Rush package at <u>Sky Combat Ace (SCA)</u> located at the Henderson Executive Airport. This aerial combat experience, in a high tech 330 horsepower Extra 330LC aircraft, is guaranteed to be one hell of a thrill ride.

Another experience for the brave is the controlled free-fall at <u>Sky Jump</u> Las Vegas. This little adventure will help you get over any fear of heights as you take an 855-foot plunge off the <u>Stratosphere</u> (you are actually on a cable jumping off the 108th floor). This ride is guaranteed to pump a few ounces of adrenaline into the veins. The view at night is incredible.

To prepare for the Stratosphere jump, a little time in the skydiving simulator at <u>Vegas Indoor Skydiving</u> might help to prepare you for the real thing. This is an experience worth an hour of your time.

If you are in the "need for speed" take a visit to <u>Dream Racing</u> and hop into a Ferrari F430 GT, a Lamborghini, or any number of exotic cars. A five-lap spin will cost on the order of five bills. Or you can spend a little time in the simulator. Dream Racing is located at the Las Vegas Motor Speedway. 7000 Las Vegas Blvd. N. Las Vegas, Nevada 89115. (702) 605-3000.

Should driving a NASCAR car be one of your dreams, the <u>Richard Petty Driving Experience</u> is also located at the Las Vegas Speedway. This is where you can get the feel for what 600 horsepower can really do; or for the more timid, you can take a 165 mph ride with a professional.

If you'd like to put yourself into a James Bond movie, try an Aston Martin Vantage S at <u>Exotics Racing,</u> also at the Las Vegas Motor Speedway. They have a fine selection of Lamborghini and Ferrari supercars and up to <u>14 exotic cars</u>. You could even take that Blond Russian Knockout along for the ride and some cool photos.

If you like Iron Man, then you might be interested in seeing how pulling a few levers can move a ton of dirt around. <u>Dig This</u> is one of the unique attractions in Las Vegas where you can test your skills at operating a big tractor. Dig This is located at 3012 S. Rancho Drive, Las Vegas. 888-344-8447.

For an off road experience, <u>VORE (Vegas Off Road Experience)</u> provides a 'behind the wheel, high speed, in the air, helmet included' day of fun.

16
PHOTOGRAPHY

L as Vegas is a cool city for photography, especially for night photos around Nautical Dusk. If you want a good app for your smart phone, get <u>Sol: Sun Clock</u>. This app indicates when the Golden Hour PM, Civil Dusk, Nautical Dusk, and Astronomical Dusk begin and end. You can set an alarm, which is especially useful when you are indoors. This is a good app to remind you when you may want to be at your favorite location for picture taking.

Another good app is <u>Sun Surveyor Lite</u>. This app has a unique 3D compass feature that shows the angle of the sun at any particular time of day. Should you want to return to a favorite place when shade is just right for a particular scene, this is the app for you. You can also check for the same sun angle on any calendar date in the future, or you can go back and see what the angle was for any past date. This app is especially valuable for taking pictures along the Las Vegas Strip, and it shows Civil, Nautical, and Astronomical Dusk.

UNIQUE PLACES FOR PHOTOS IN LAS VEGAS

A great photo can be taken from the <u>Stratosphere Tower</u> at Nautical Dusk, which is the period when the sky turns deep blue and the city lights are on. Be warned that tripods are not allowed at the observation deck, so plan in advance for getting that perfect shot. This is the best location for a view looking south of the Strip. A window seat at the <u>Top of the World Restaurant</u> also provides some good opportunities.

<u>The Foundation Room</u> and the <u>Mix Lounge</u> at the top of Mandalay Bay both offer a near panoramic view of the Strip from

every seat. This location towers 400 feet above the desert floor and offers one of the best opportunities for astounding photos. Tripods are not allowed, but the outdoor terrace offers the advantage of no windows with reflections, and there is a nice rail to steady your camera. The view is looking north up the Strip with a good shot of the Paris Hotel. The Foundation Room has a dress code.

The Voodoo Rooftop Nightclub on top of the Rio Hotel offers a stunning panoramic view of the Strip. The outdoor patio access from the bar provides an unencumbered view of most of the West side of the Strip. No tripods are allowed, but there are a number of good railings to steady your camera. It is no wonder that this is the top proposal spot in Las Vegas.

The Terminal 1 Parking Structure at McCarran Airport offers one of the best east side views of the Strip. This is especially good during fireworks displays such as New Years and Fourth of July. Drive to the Terminal 1 Short Term Parking Structure and park in short term parking as if you were waiting for passenger pickup. Take the elevator or stairway up to an upper level. The northwest corner of the structure offers an incredible view. Don't forget to take your tripod!

The High Roller is another spot that rates high on the list. It is fun to photograph the observation wheel from the ground in the LINQ area and from the passenger cabs. See The High Roller in Chapter 17.

17
SOME FUN THINGS TO DO

If you are interested in doing some interesting activities away from the Strip that only the locals seem to know about, there are many great options.

THE LANDINGS CAFÉ
HENDERSON EXECUTIVE AIRPORT

The Landings Café is located south of Las Vegas just east of the M Hotel at the Henderson Executive Airport. You can enjoy a relaxing time here at the local hang out, enjoy breakfast, or lunch, with a chance of rubbing shoulders with private jet owners. The food is great and the owner, Marie, will most likely be there to make your dining experience most pleasurable.

Of course, if you are "Leaving Las Vegas In Style" in your own rented jet, Chapter 19, you might want to stop in at the Landings Café for a departing breakfast. The Landings has some decent ratings at Trip Advisor and positive reviews on Yelp.

RUNNING TAIL NUMBERS
AT THE EXECUTIVE AIRPORT

While dining at the Landings Café, you can pass idle time by Running Tail Numbers, an unexpectedly entertaining activity. Using Flight Aware's live flight tracking and code HND (for the Henderson Executive Airport) you can see what aircraft are arriving and leaving, and see where they have been, and where they are going.

It is as easy as typing in the "N" number of an aircraft into the little box and hitting return. With a little practice, you will be able to tell whose private jet is coming in by looking at the aircraft registration history, and if your camera is ready, you might even get a photo of the passengers transferring from their private jet to a limousine.

Running Tail Number Example: A 3-engine jet with a cool logo on the tail (skull with top hat) and number N500TS. This is a Falcon 50 Jet owned by True Speed Enterprises II, Inc. Do a Google search for True Speed Enterprises II, Inc. and you will find a corporate listing for Tony Stewart the NASCAR driver.

MUSEUMS

An extensive listing of museums in Las Vegas can be found on the Las Vegas Tourism website. One that is highly recommended is the Atomic Test Museum, a history packed one-of-a-kind place. The National Atomic Test Museum offers exhibits on the history of nuclear weapons and runs videos of some incredible above ground tests. If you are interested in the history of WWII, or grew up during the cold war era, this museum should not be missed. The Atomic Test Museum also has one of the most extensive databases of information on Area 51. The museum is located a few blocks east of the Strip at 755 E. Flamingo Rd. Las Vegas, Nevada 702-794-5151.

Take your gambling winnings to the Quad Hotel and Casino and buy yourself a vintage automobile at the Auto Collections. This is one of the most unusual things to do in Las Vegas; the attraction combines the thrills of an exotic car museum with the opportunity to actually buy some of the most unique and eclectic automobiles in the world. This is a jaw dropping experience for any automobile buff.

A good place to visit for a couple hours is The Mob Museum where all the big names associated with crime, and fighting crime, are included. This is a fascinating place for anyone interested in the crime history of America. It is located at 300 Stewart Avenue, a few blocks west of Fremont Street. 702-229-2734.

SPAS

The <u>Episage wellness center</u> is one spa not located in a hotel that has some excellent <u>Trip Advisor Reviews</u>. It is a favorite among the locals.

If you are looking for a standard, good standby massage you cannot go wrong with <u>Elements Massage in Summerlin,</u> or <u>Elements in Henderson</u>. Appointments are recommended.

<u>My Spa</u> is a local massage business located on S. Eastern in Henderson. Linda, the owner, is a licensed massage therapist; she has worked under a Chinese doctor and specializes in pain management. She does deep tissue massage that will work out the pain. You can expect a massage with a Chinese twist (she is as good with her feet as she is with her hands). A massage at My Spa is very enjoyable and affordable. Plan on at least 90 minutes. This is one of the best massages for the money.

<u>Encore Spa at the Wynn</u> is a top-of-the-line spa with excellent <u>Trip Advisor reviews</u>.

<u>Qua Baths & Spa</u> is located in Caesar's Place and gets consistently high <u>reviews</u> for an enjoyable experience.

<u>Boracay Massage</u> is another local spa, located off the Strip on the west side of the valley; it specializes in massages for couples. Boracay Massage has been in business for 17 years and caters mostly to tourists. They are located 7 miles from the MGM Grand, just off W. Tropicana and Highway 215. This small location inside a strip-mall gets <u>excellent reviews</u> and is worth a visit. Reservations required.

GYMS

If you want to see where all the entertainers go to work out, check out <u>Las Vegas Athletic Clubs</u> in the early to mid afternoons. The clubs on Flamingo Road and Eastern Ave enjoy a high bias of entertainers. Club Day passes are available for $20 and weekly passes are $50. There is a great Starbucks Coffee Shop next to the Eastern Ave Club where many entertainers go for a healthy cup of tea post workout.

THE HIGH ROLLER

The High Roller is the tallest observation wheel in the world at 550 feet above the ground. Located between the Quad and the Flamingo Hotels in the LINQ area, the High Roller offers an easy walk on entry and walk off exit while the wheel is rotating. When one enters one of the 40-person, 22-ton, air conditioned passenger cabins, only then does the size of the wheel and the incredible engineering behind it become apparent. This thing is huge and it becomes bigger in the mind as one enjoys the 30-minute rotation period and the splendid view. At night, the 7.3 million pound observation wheel becomes a pallet of changing colors, which only adds to the grandiose lighting of the surrounding city. This is an excellent place for photographs. Schedule a dinner, party, or a wedding for a revolution ride that will be memorable. This is a definite must do experience. Tickets start at $24.95 for daytime and $34.95 for nighttime rides.

GRAND CANYON TOURS

Maverick Aviation Group offers some of the best Grand Canyon Tours out of Las Vegas. With over 40 helicopters and airplanes they offer a number of exciting tour packages to meet the needs of any Las Vegas tourist. From evening flights to view the lights of the city to visiting the Colorado River deep in the Grand Canyon, they have plenty of exciting rides to choose from.

18
MARRIAGE AND DIVORCE

Getting married in Las Vegas is a unique experience to say the least; whether it is a "drive through wedding" or a "helicopter wedding," there are many weddings taking place in the city of lights.

Las Vegas weddings started out as cheap, fast, and easy weddings for those that wanted to dash away from Los Angeles for the weekend without anyone knowing. Regardless of how or when the ceremonies are performed, it is important to know that they are real and they are final.

MARRIAGE

<u>Las Vegas Weddings</u> can be easy. Acquiring a marriage license in Las Vegas is a straightforward and simple process. No blood test or waiting period is required. Marriage applicants must be a biological male and biological female, though this may be changing.

Once a short form is completed and submitted to the Bureau, along with $60 cash and a government issued photo ID, a marriage license may be obtained within minutes. Within one year of receipt of the marriage license, a wedding ceremony must be performed in order to have a legal union.

The Las Vegas Tourism website provides a good overview of marriage requirements that might be worthwhile to review before tying the knot.

Here are the Clark County Requirements for marriage and the on-line pre-marriage application.

For those that are interested in the "fine print" on marriage, here is the Nevada Revised Statutes For Marriage in the State of Nevada.

There are many places to get married in Las Vegas, but for a starter there are some good tips at Vegas.com for those that are in a hurry.

If you are thinking about tying the knot, why not also plan your bachelor or bachelorette party in Las Vegas? See Chapter 6 Entertainment Clubs.

DIVORCE

Should you wake up one morning in Las Vegas wondering, "What the Hell Happened Last Night?" you might end up needing to get a divorce. Nevada is a no fault divorce state. The most common grounds for divorce in Nevada are incompatibility.

To get a divorce, even uncontested, you need to be a resident of Clark County for at least 6 weeks before filing papers. If the divorce is uncontested, both spouses sign the Joint Petition for Divorce in front of a Notary Public. One spouse files the documents with the District Court Clerk and pays the filing fee.

After filing the papers, if there are no complications, the Divorce Decree will be signed by the judge and in 3 to 6 weeks the divorce is final.

Nevada law considers the state, and the cities like Las Vegas within it, to be "community property jurisdictions." Community property issues can be complicated and one is advised to see an attorney who is familiar with this area of the law.

If you decide to go forward with a divorce, here is a good summary page titled <u>Divorces In Nevada</u> that will get you started for as little at $89. And to make it easier, you can <u>complete your Nevada divorce online</u>.

Just to make sure you know all the fine print, here is the <u>Nevada Revised Statutes for Dissolution of Marriage</u>.

Well, it's over. So what to do? Throw a divorce party! See Chapter 6 Entertainment Clubs.

19
LEAVING LAS VEGAS IN STYLE

If you flew into Las Vegas and you want to leave with class, why not rent your own private jet? Bypass that Medusa Seductress out there on the four-hour drive back to LA and leave Las Vegas when you want to.

If you are in a group of six people, for $1,000 each, you can rent a private jet back to California. You will be flown to a small airport near where you live, or directly to LAX or SFO for your commercial flight home.

Take a limousine ride from your hotel to the Henderson Executive Airport, bypass security, and go directly to your airplane. Take some great pictures next to your jet. Don't forget your video camera!

Lucky Jets is a Las Vegas based company, and you get the royal local service when you schedule. Sometimes they can react with only a few hours notice, but it is better if you can give them a couple days lead-time.

If you want to add a little fun, take your limo to the airport, enjoy breakfast at the Landings (they open at 7AM), and take a nice stroll out to your jet. If you go a little earlier, you can meet the astronomical dawn and get a few priceless sunrise photos of the lighted city on your way out.

Other Jet Charter Companies that can arrange jet services out of McCarran International Airport or Henderson Executive Airport are:

116

Las Vegas VIP Entertainment, a one-stop service for booking private jets and everything else that you can imagine. They can be reached at 702-530-7713.

Two other jet rental companies to check out are Cirrus Aviation at 702-448-2366, and NV Jets at 702-798-7001.

Now that's the way to leave Las Vegas in Style!

APPENDIX A
MAPS

LAS VEGAS METROPOLITAN AREA

General Las Vegas Metropolitan Area information is available on Wikipedia.

The metropolitan area includes Las Vegas, Clark County, and the City of Henderson. The boundaries map includes the entire metropolitan area including the unincorporated areas.

A larger more detailed Las Vegas Metro Area map is available from the City of Las Vegas web page.

A faster interactive map of Las Vegas is available from Las Vegas Tourism. This map shows detail down to street level with hotels and points of interest identified.

Additionally, tourists can pick up a Las Vegas folded map provided by the Las Vegas Tourism at any brochure stand, which also shows excellent detail of the Strip.

The "Strip," along Las Vegas Blvd, runs from I-215 at McCarran Airport up to Sahara Blvd and is situated in the unincorporated city of Paradise in Clark County. It is not situated in the City of Las Vegas or the City of North Las Vegas, as many mistakenly believe. The Strip falls under the jurisdiction of the Las Vegas Metropolitan Police Department.

CITY OF LAS VEGAS

General information about the City of Las Vegas is available on Wikipedia. An excellent Interactive map of Las Vegas is the first map on the City of Las Vegas maps page. This is one of the most useful maps with boundaries of the cities of Las Vegas and Henderson.

CLARK COUNTY

General information about Clark County is available on Wikipedia.

The Metropolitan area of Las Vegas map is downloadable only, and shows the boundaries of the cities of Las Vegas, North Las Vegas, and Henderson. This map also shows areas that fall within the jurisdiction of Clark County.

The Clark County maps section provides very poor maps, especially for interactive purposes. The downloadable maps are very slow loading, but they are useful for those who need them.

The following links are for the general locations in the greater Las Vegas Metropolitan Area and in Clark County.

North Las Vegas – is an incorporated city located to the north of the Strip. North Las Vegas City laws apply here as well as Clark County laws.

> Paradise – is an unincorporated city that includes the Strip. Clark County laws apply.
>
> Enterprise – is an unincorporated city located south of the Strip and west of McCarran International Airport. Clark County laws apply.
>
> Spring Valley – is an unincorporated city located west of the Strip that includes Chinatown. Clark County Laws apply.
>
> Sunrise Manor – is an unincorporated city located to the east of the Strip. Clark County Laws apply.
>
> Winchester – is an unincorporated city located to the east of the Strip that includes part of the Strip. Clark County laws apply.

CITY OF HENDERSON

General information about City of Henderson is available on Wikipedia.

The City of Henderson is an incorporated city located to the south of the Strip. City of Henderson laws are applicable here as well as those of Clark County.

The City of Henderson has excellent <u>Henderson City Limits Maps</u> suitable for downloading that can be zoomed in on to show boundaries at the street level. Some of these maps will require the latest Flash Player to operate.

A Henderson City Limits Map can be downloaded from the cities Geographic Information Services, (<u>GIS</u>) web page.

BOULDER CITY

General information about <u>Boulder City</u> is available on Wikipedia.

Printable maps of Boulder City are available on the <u>Boulder City maps website</u>.

APPENDIX B
LAWS AND
ORDINANCES

Disclaimer: *This book is a reference manual and tour guide for adult activities in and around Las Vegas, Nevada and is based upon opinions gathered and concluded by the author. The author is not an attorney and is not attempting to or qualified to practice law or give legal advice. The various statutes have been provided in this book for your reference and may not be current or complete. It is strongly recommended that you seek legal advice from a qualified professional familiar with the area of law you are concerned with before engaging in any activities that may be subject to legal interpretation. In that regard, please note that the author neither recommends nor endorses any attorney or any group of attorneys; it is strictly up to you, the reader, to obtain suitable legal advice from a professional based upon the reader's interview and review of competency of that individual or firm.*

LAWS AND ORDINANCES

The following codes and ordinances apply to the Las Vegas Metro and surrounding area:

> State of Nevada – Nevada Revised Statutes
> Clark County – Code of Ordinances that apply
>   in Clark County areas unless superseded by
>   City Codes within the county
> City of Las Vegas Codes
> City of North Las Vegas Codes
> City of Henderson Codes
> Boulder City Codes

STATE OF NEVADA

The Nevada Revised Statutes are the general laws applying in the State of Nevada. The **Nevada Revised Statutes** can be found on the State of Nevada Revised Statutes website.

General Crimes are listed under Title 15 – Crimes and Punishments. Most laws that tourists in Las Vegas will be concerned with appear to be under this Title and are covered in Chapters 200 through 207; for controlled substances see Chapter 453.

Section 200.364 – Sexual Assault and Seduction: Definitions

As used in NRS 200.364 to 200.3784, inclusive, unless the context otherwise requires:

1. "Offense involving a pupil" means any of the following offenses:

   (a) Sexual conduct between certain employees of a school or volunteers at a school and a pupil pursuant to NRS 201.540.

   (b) Sexual conduct between certain employees of a college or university and a student pursuant to NRS 201.550.

2. "Perpetrator" means a person who commits a sexual offense, an offense involving a pupil or sex trafficking.

3. "Sex trafficking" means a violation of subsection 2 of NRS 201.300.

4. "Sexual offense" means any of the following offenses:

   (a) Sexual assault pursuant to NRS 200.366.

   (b) Statutory sexual seduction pursuant to NRS 200.368.

5. "Sexual penetration" means cunnilingus, fellatio, or any intrusion, however slight, of any part of a person's body or any object manipulated or inserted by a person into the genital or anal openings of the body of another, including sexual intercourse in its ordinary meaning.

6. "Statutory sexual seduction" means:

    (a) Ordinary sexual intercourse, anal intercourse, cunnilingus or fellatio committed by a person 18 years of age or older with a person under the age of 16 years; or

    (b) Any other sexual penetration committed by a person 18 years of age or older with a person under the age of 16 years with the intent of arousing, appealing to, or gratifying the lust or passions or sexual desires of either of the persons.

7. "Victim" means a person who is a victim of a sexual offense, an offense involving a pupil, or sex trafficking.

Added to NRS by 1977, 1626; A 1979, 572; 1991, 801; 1995, 700; 2009, 231, 1296; 2013, 2426

Section 200.366 — Sexual Assault: Definition; penalties

1. A person who subjects another person to sexual penetration, or who forces another person to make a sexual penetration on himself or herself or another, or on a beast, against the will of the victim or under conditions in which the perpetrator knows or should know that the victim is mentally or physically incapable of resisting or understanding the nature of his or her conduct, is guilty of sexual assault.

2. Except as otherwise provided in subsections 3 and 4, a person who commits a sexual assault is guilty of a category A felony and shall be punished:

    (a) If substantial bodily harm to the victim results from the actions of the defendant committed in connection with or as a part of the sexual assault, by imprisonment in the state prison:

        (1) For life without the possibility of parole; or

        (2) For life with the possibility of parole, with eligibility for parole beginning when a minimum of 15 years has been served.

(b) If no substantial bodily harm to the victim results, by imprisonment in the state prison for life with the possibility of parole, with eligibility for parole beginning when a minimum of 10 years has been served.

3. Except as otherwise provided in subsection 4, a person who commits a sexual assault against a child under the age of 16 years is guilty of a category A felony and shall be punished:

(a) If the crime results in substantial bodily harm to the child, by imprisonment in the state prison for life without the possibility of parole.

(b) Except as otherwise provided in paragraph (c), if the crime does not result in substantial bodily harm to the child, by imprisonment in the state prison for life with the possibility of parole, with eligibility for parole beginning when a minimum of 25 years has been served.

(c) If the crime is committed against a child under the age of 14 years and does not result in substantial bodily harm to the child, by imprisonment in the state prison for life with the possibility of parole, with eligibility for parole beginning when a minimum of 35 years has been served.

4. A person who commits a sexual assault against a child under the age of 16 years and who has been previously convicted of:

(a) A sexual assault pursuant to this section or any other sexual offense against a child; or

(b) An offense committed in another jurisdiction that, if committed in this State, would constitute a sexual assault pursuant to this section or any other sexual offense against a child, is guilty of a category A felony and shall be punished by imprisonment in the state prison for life without the possibility of parole.

5. For the purpose of this section, "other sexual offense against a child" means any act committed by an adult upon a child constituting:

   (a) Incest pursuant to NRS 201.180;

   (b) Lewdness with a child pursuant to NRS 201.230;

   (c) Sado-masochistic abuse pursuant to NRS 201.262; or

   (d) Luring a child using a computer, system or network pursuant to NRS 201.560, if punished as a felony.

Added to NRS by 1977, 1626; A 1991, 612; 1995, 1186; 1997, 1179, 1719; 1999, 431; 2003, 2825; 2005, 2874; 2007, 3255

NRS 201.210 — Open and Gross Lewdness

1. A person who commits any act of open or gross lewdness is guilty:

   (a) For the first offense, of a gross misdemeanor.

   (b) For any subsequent offense, of a category D felony and shall be punished as provided in NRS 193.130.

2. For the purposes of this section, the breast-feeding of a child by the mother of the child does not constitute an act of open or gross lewdness.

[Part 1911 C&P § 195; A 1921, 112; NCL § 10142] — NRS A 1963, 63; 1965, 1465; 1967, 476; 1973, 95, 255, 1406; 1977, 866; 1979, 1429; 1983, 206; 1991, 1008; 1995, 127, 1199, 1327; 1997, 2501, 3188

NRS 193.130 — Categories and punishment of felonies

1. Except when a person is convicted of a category A felony, and except as otherwise provided by specific statute, a person convicted of a felony shall be sentenced to a minimum term and a maximum term of imprisonment which must be within the limits prescribed by the applicable statute, unless the statute in force at the time of commission of the felony prescribed a different penalty. The minimum term of imprisonment that may be imposed must not exceed 40 percent of the maximum term imposed.

2. Except as otherwise provided by specific statute, for each felony committed on or after July 1, 1995:

(a) A category A felony is a felony for which a sentence of death or imprisonment in the state prison for life with or without the possibility of parole may be imposed, as provided by specific statute.

(b) A category B felony is a felony for which the minimum term of imprisonment in the state prison that may be imposed is not less than 1 year and the maximum term of imprisonment that may be imposed is not more than 20 years, as provided by specific statute.

(c) A category C felony is a felony for which a court shall sentence a convicted person to imprisonment in the state prison for a minimum term of not less than 1 year and a maximum term of not more than 5 years. In addition to any other penalty, the court may impose a fine of not more than $10,000, unless a greater fine is authorized or required by statute.

(d) A category D felony is a felony for which a court shall sentence a convicted person to imprisonment in the state prison for a minimum term of not less than 1 year and a maximum term of not more than 4 years. In addition to any other penalty, the court may impose a fine of not more than $5,000, unless a greater fine is authorized or required by statute.

(e) A category E felony is a felony for which a court shall sentence a convicted person to imprisonment in the state prison for a minimum term of not less than 1 year and a maximum term of not more than 4 years. Except as otherwise provided in paragraph (b) of subsection 1 of NRS 176A.100, upon sentencing a person who is found guilty of a category E felony, the court shall suspend the execution of the sentence and grant probation to the person upon such conditions as the court deems appropriate. Such conditions of probation may include, but are not limited to, requiring the person to serve a term of confinement of not more than 1 year in the county jail. In addition to any other penalty, the court may impose a fine of not more than $5,000, unless a greater penalty is authorized or required by statute.

[1911 C&P § 18; RL § 6283; NCL § 9967] — NRS A 1967, 458; 1995, 1167; 1997, 1177; 1999, 1186

NRS 244.345 — Dancing halls, escort services, entertainment by referral services and gambling games or devices; limitation on licensing of houses of prostitution.

1. Every natural person wishing to be employed as an entertainer for an entertainment by referral service and every natural person, firm, association of persons or corporation wishing to engage in the business of conducting a dancing hall, escort service, entertainment by referral service or gambling game or device permitted by law, outside of an incorporated city, must:

   (a) Make application to the license board of the county in which the employment or business is to be engaged in, for a county license of the kind desired. The application must be in a form prescribed by the regulations of the license board.

   (b) File the application with the required license fee with the county license collector, as provided in chapter 364 of NRS, who shall present the application to the license board at its next regular meeting. The board, in counties whose population is less than 700,000, may refer the petition to the sheriff, who shall report upon it at the following regular meeting of the board. In counties whose population is 700,000 or more, the board shall refer the petition to the metropolitan police department. The department shall conduct an investigation relating to the petition and report its findings to the board at the next regular meeting of the board. The board shall at that meeting grant or refuse the license prayed for or enter any other order consistent with its regulations. Except in the case of an application for a license to conduct a gambling game or device, the county license collector may grant a temporary permit to an applicant, valid only until the next regular meeting of the board. In unincorporated towns and cities governed pursuant to the provisions of chapter 269 of NRS, the license board has the exclusive power to license and regulate the employment and businesses mentioned in this subsection.

2. The board of county commissioners, and in a county whose population is less than 700,000, the sheriff of that county constitute the license board, and the county clerk or other person designated by the license board is the clerk thereof, in the respective counties of this state.

3. The license board may, without further compensation to the board or its clerk:

   (a) Fix, impose and collect license fees upon the employment and businesses mentioned in this section.

   (b) Grant or deny applications for licenses and impose conditions, limitations and restrictions upon the licensee.

   (c) Adopt, amend and repeal regulations relating to licenses and licensees.

   (d) Restrict, revoke or suspend licenses for cause after hearing. In an emergency the board may issue an order for immediate suspension or limitation of a license, but the order must state the reason for suspension or limitation and afford the licensee a hearing.

4. The license board shall hold a hearing before adopting proposed regulations, before adopting amendments to regulations, and before repealing regulations relating to the control or the licensing of the employment or businesses mentioned in this section. Notice of the hearing

must be published in a newspaper published and having general circulation in the county at least once a week for 2 weeks before the hearing.

5. Upon adoption of new regulations the board shall designate their effective date, which may not be earlier than 15 days after their adoption. Immediately after adoption a copy of any new regulations must be available for public inspection during regular business hours at the office of the county clerk.

6. Except as otherwise provided in NRS 241.0355, a majority of the members constitutes a quorum for the transaction of business.

7. Any natural person, firm, association of persons or corporation who engages in the employment of any of the businesses mentioned in this section without first having obtained the license and paid the license fee as provided in this section is guilty of a misdemeanor.

8. In a county whose population is 700,000 or more, the license board shall not grant any license to a petitioner for the purpose of operating a house of ill fame or repute or any other business employing any person for the purpose of prostitution.

9. As used in this section:

    (a) "Entertainer for an entertainment by referral service" means a natural person who is sent or referred for a fee to a hotel or motel room, home or other accommodation by an entertainment by referral service for the purpose of entertaining the person located in the hotel or motel room, home or other accommodation.

    (b) "Entertainment by referral service" means a person or group of persons who send or refer another person to a hotel or motel room, home or other accommodation for a fee in response to a telephone or other request for the purpose of entertaining the person located in the hotel or motel room, home or other accommodation.

[1:50:1923; NCL § 2037] + [2:50:1923; NCL § 2038] + [3:50:1923; NCL § 2039] + [4:50:1923; NCL § 2040] — NRS A 1959, 838; 1961, 364; 1971, 11; 1973, 923; 1975, 562; 1979, 20, 305, 511, 728, 730, 732, 733; 1989, 1899; 1991, 166; 2001, 1124; 2011, 1105

NRS Chapter 453 — Controlled Substances

NRS 453.043 — "Controlled substance analog" defined.

1. "Controlled substance analog" means a substance the chemical structure of which is substantially similar to the chemical structure of a controlled substance placed in schedule I or II and:

   (a) Which has a stimulant, depressant or hallucinogenic effect on the central nervous system substantially similar to the stimulant, depressant or hallucinogenic effect on the central nervous system of a controlled substance placed in schedule I or II pursuant to NRS 453.166 or NRS 453.176; or

   (b) With respect to a particular person, which he or she represents or intends to have a stimulant, depressant or hallucinogenic effect on the central nervous system substantially similar to the stimulant, depressant or hallucinogenic effect on the central nervous system of a controlled substance included in schedule I or II.

2. The term does not include:

   (a) A controlled substance;

   (b) A substance for which there is an approved new drug application;

   (c) A substance with respect to which an exemption is in effect for investigational use by a particular person under Section 505 of the federal Food, Drug, and Cosmetic Act (21 U.S.C. § 355) to the extent conduct with respect to the substance is permitted by the exemption; or

   (d) Any substance to the extent not intended for human

consumption before an exemption takes effect with respect to the substance.

Added to NRS by 1991 Statutes, Page 1644

COMMON MISDEMEANOR CHARGES NEVADA STATUTES

1. Assault (NRS 200.471) – Intentionally placing another person in reasonable apprehension of immediate bodily harm. (No touching needs to take place.)

2. Battery (NRS 200.390) – Any willful and unlawful use of force or violence upon the person of another.

3. Driving Under the Influence/DUI (NRS Chapter 484C) – Operating a motor vehicle under the influence of drugs or alcohol.

4. Petit Theft (NRS 205.0821) – A person who without lawful authority knowingly controls any property of another person with the intent to deprive that person of that property. The theft is considered a misdemeanor where the value of the property is not greater than $250.

5. Local Drug Possession (NRS 453.336) – Any person within the state of Nevada who possesses any drug, which may not be lawfully introduced into interstate commerce under the Federal Food, Drug, and Cosmetic Act, is guilty of a misdemeanor.

6. Prostitution (NRS 201.354) – A male or female person who for a fee engages in sexual intercourse, oral genital contact, or any touching of the sexual organs or other intimate parts of a person for the purpose of arousing or gratifying the sexual desire of either person is guilty of a misdemeanor.

7. Trespass (NRS 207.200) – A person who goes upon the land or into any building of another with the intent to vex or annoy the owner or occupant or a person willfully goes or remains upon the land or in any building after having been warned by the owner or occupant thereof not to trespass is guilty of a misdemeanor.

8. Vandalism (NRS Chapter 205) – Intentional and malicious criminal damage to property.

9. Shoplifting (NRS 205.0832) – Taking the property of another without permission with the intent of permanently depriving the owner of the property.

10. Resisting Arrest (NRS 199.280) – Falls under the category of battery, but the difference is that a police officer is the victim of a physical attack. Resisting arrest charges could also stem from running away (fleeing) from an officer on foot or in a vehicle.

11. Traffic Tickets (NRS 484) – Nevada law has a wide array of traffic violations such as speeding, non-moving violations, parking violations, driving on a suspended license, and failure to wear a seatbelt.

12. Driving while Texting, Phoning, or Using other Electronic Devices – (NRS 484B.165) – Using your cellular phone or other electronic device while operating a moving vehicle.

CLARK COUNTY

Clark County Code of Ordinances Library

Chapter 6.140 - Outcall Promoters and Entertainers
Chapter 6.140.140 - Outcall Regulations
Chapter 6.140.150 - Prostitution Unlawful
Chapter 7.08 - Massage Industry
Chapter 7.54 - Sexually Oriented Commercial Enterprises

12.04.180 - Concealed weapons prohibited without permit.
It is unlawful within the unincorporated area of Clark County for any person to carry upon his person a concealed weapon of any description, including a knife with a blade of three inches or more, a gun, pistol, revolver or other firearm capable of being concealed without first having received written permission therefore from the sheriff.
Chapter 12.04.200 - Registration of firearms capable of being concealed.

It is unlawful for any person with at least sixty days of residency in the county to own or have in his possession, within the unincorporated area of Clark County, a pistol or other firearm capable of being concealed, unless the same has first been registered with the sheriff or with a police department of any of the incorporated cities of Clark County.

(Ord. 3571 § 4, 2007: Ord. 242 § 20, 1965)

CITY OF LAS VEGAS
City of Las Vegas Municipal Codes Library

CITY OF NORTH LAS VEGAS
City of North Las Vegas Municipal Codes Library
Chapter 9.16 - Controlled Substances

CITY OF HENDERSON
City of Henderson Municipal Codes Library
Section 04.84 - Massage Establishments and Independent Massage Therapists
Section 04.85 - Reflexology

BOULDER CITY
Boulder City Municipal Codes Library
Title 4 - Chapter 10 - Massage Technicians and Massage Centers

APPENDIX C
GUNS

Disclaimer: *The Laws and Statutes cited herein are by no means all-inclusive and are not to be given absolute credence. The few that are cited are to provide the reader with a small understanding of the seriousness of the laws, and serve as a starting place for further reading. It is strongly recommended that you seek legal advice from a qualified professional familiar with the area of law you are concerned with before engaging in any activities that may be subject to legal interpretation. Readers should investigate thoroughly the laws that apply to guns prior to their use in the State of Nevada, Clark County, or the cities of Las Vegas, North Las Vegas, or Henderson.*

NEVADA REVISED STATUTES ON GUNS

<u>NRS 202.253</u> **Weapons – Dangerous Weapons and Firearms**

<u>NRS 202.3653</u> **Concealed Firearms**

<u>NRS 202.320</u> **Drawing deadly weapon in threatening manner.**

1. Unless a greater penalty is provided in <u>NRS 202.287</u> (Discharging firearms within or from structures or vehicles; penalties) a person having, carrying or procuring from another person any dirk, dirk-knife, sword, sword cane, pistol, gun or other deadly weapon, who, in the presence of two or more persons, draws or exhibits any of such deadly weapons in a rude, angry or threatening manner not in necessary self-defense, or who in any manner unlawfully uses that weapon in any fight or quarrel, is guilty of a misdemeanor.

2. A sheriff, deputy sheriff, marshal, constable or other peace officer shall not be held to answer, under the provisions of subsection 1, for drawing or exhibiting any of the weapons mentioned therein while in the lawful discharge of his or her duties.

[1911 C&P § 174; RL § 6439; NCL § 10121] — (NRS A 1967, 486; 1989, 1240)

NORTH LAS VEGAS GUN LAWS

Chapter 9.32 Weapons Generally

Chapter 9.36 Pistols

CLARK COUNTY GUN LAWS

12.04.230 Discharging unlawful — Exceptions

It is unlawful to willfully discharge any pistol, firearm, air gun, musket or instrument of any kind, character or description which throws a bullet or missile of any kind for any distance by means of the elastic force of air or any explosive substance within that area legally described below and depicted by the shaded areas on the map labeled Attachment A, adopted herewith as signed and dated by the chairman of the board of county commissioners and available for public inspection in the commission division office of the county clerk.

The areas in the county where it is unlawful to willfully discharge a firearm, excluding shooting ranges, or a sanctioned event by federal, state, county or an incorporated city currently licensed by business license, are generally located within the entire unincorporated towns of Whitney, Paradise, Spring Valley, Sunrise Manor [,] and Winchester [and Goodsprings], the urbanized areas of Lone Mountain and Enterprise, Sandy Valley, Blue Diamond, Calico Basin, the area south of State Route 157 in Section 1 and all of Section 12, Township 19 South, Range 59 East, the proposed Apex Heavy Industry Zone, Las Vegas Dunes Recreation Area, the Sunrise Mountain Natural Area, Rainbow

Gardens and the River Mountain area between Henderson, and the Lake Mead Recreation Area north of Boulder Highway.

SHOOTING CLOSURE AREAS

Shooting closure areas around Las Vegas are shown on two maps. The <u>Las Vegas Valley Target Shooting Closure Map</u> shows the closed areas around Las Vegas and the <u>Pahrump Closure Map</u> shows the newly established closure area south of Pahrump just west of Las Vegas. Before embarking on a desert-shooting outing, it is highly recommended to visit a local government office to see if the area of interest is in a closure area.

APPENDIX D
PROSTITUTION
AND DRUGS
CALCULATIONS

Disclaimer: *Some interesting results can be viewed if facts from various sources are correct and interpreted correctly. The calculations that follow concerning prostitution and drugs are based in part on facts gathered from various sources and interpreted to present the seriousness, pervasiveness and prevalence of the problems and are not to be given absolute credence.*

PROSTITUTION CALCULATION

For calculations, the average population of Las Vegas (2 million), including tourists (405,479), is estimated to be 2,405,479. The tourist population was calculated as follows: 40 million tourists x 3.7 nights/365 days per year = 405, 479 tourists for a year.

Prostitution is not legal in Las Vegas, however it is legal in Nye County. Therefore, by definition, Las Vegas does not have prostitutes. However, Las Vegas has escorts, entertainers, massage therapists, etc.

Of these, there are Men Offering Adult Needs, Ladies Offering Adult Needs, Persons Offering Licentious Entertainment, and all of these together might be classified as Professional Entertainers Offering Prurient Licentious Entertainment (PEOPLE).

In sum, Las Vegas doesn't have prostitutes, but it has many sex workers, or PEOPLE. So, how many PEOPLE are working in Las Vegas? After interviewing hundreds of people in the industry including law enforcement, the following assumptions were made:

PEOPLE working at major hotels = 200, at minor hotels = 100, with fewer at the remainder hotels. Number of hotels in Las Vegas area = 150.

Strip Major Hotels 10 x 200 = 2,000 PEOPLE

Strip Minor Hotels 10 x 100 = 1,000 PEOPLE

Strip Smaller Hotels 32 x 25 = 800 PEOPLE

South Strip Hotels 22 x 25 = 550 PEOPLE

Fremont area Hotels 14 x 25 = 350 PEOPLE

Summerland Hotels 5 x 5 = 25 PEOPLE

East of Strip Hotels 32 x 5 = 160 PEOPLE

West of Strip Hotels 18 x 5 = 90 PEOPLE

Henderson Hotels 14 x 2 = 28 PEOPLE

Boulder Strip Hotels 6 x 5 = 30 PEOPLE

---

150 Hotels Subtotal = 5,033 PEOPLE

Average for 150 Hotels = 33 PEOPLE/Hotel

Assumptions from Internet:

Massage Parlors 132 x 2 = 264 PEOPLE listed as Massage Parlors

Escorts 2,091 x 1 = 2,091 PEOPLE listed on the web

In-call/Out-call Services 1,000 x 1 = 1,000 PEOPLE estimated per advertising

---

Total PEOPLE Las Vegas area = 8,388 PEOPLE working as Sex Workers. This of course does not include other venues such as street hookers and hard to quantify agency out-call PEOPLE. One might safely conclude that there are 10,000 PEOPLE working in Las Vegas.

SEX REVENUES

Assumption: Average transaction rate is $150/hr. with three transactions per 24 hours. Rates can be less and can go up to $1,000 per hour. Transactions can go to six or more per 24 hours.

If each one of these PEOPLE (sex workers) has three daily transactions at $150, the daily numbers are on the order of $3,774,600 or $113 million a month. This means the industry has revenues on the order of over $1.3 billion a year.

One may argue that Las Vegas is average in this regard and follows the statistical norm for number of PEOPLE working as Sex Workers. Wikipedia estimates this to be 23 sex workers or prostitutes per 100,000 people. For a population of 2,405,479, this equates to 577 PEOPLE in the trade in Las Vegas. If we took the "577 PEOPLE" and assume three transactions a day at $150 per transaction then we're looking at $259,650 per day, $7,789,800 a month, or nearly $94 million a year. This is still a significant industry.

When one takes a look at all the hotels and advertising associated with sex, it would be easy to extrapolate Las Vegas to ten times the national average. Therefore, we are looking at an industry on the order of a $940 million to $1 billion a year.

Let's do it another way. Escorts average about $200/hr. in the city. Legal brothels are getting roughly $1,000 per hour and the PEOPLE in the hotels are ranging from $200 to $1,000 per hour. Assume three hours of sex per PEOPLE at $200/hour or $600 per day. For the estimated 8,388 PEOPLE we get a cash flow of slightly over $5 million a day, $150 million a month, or $1.8 billion a year.

If we drop back to the 577 PEOPLE "national average," at $600 per day, we get $346,200 a day or slightly over $10 million a month, which averages a little over $126 million a year.

An excellent summary of the Sex Industry and Sex Workers in Nevada done in 2004 estimated that there were "3,000 to 3,500 indoor working PEOPLE in Las Vegas at that time." At that time, there were "100,000 registered dancers in Clark County with about 2,500 dancers working on any average day."

So, no matter how one looks at PEOPLE (Sex Workers) in Las Vegas, the industry is generating a cash flow on the order of $1.8 billion a year. On the conservative side, it is probably somewhere between $500 million to over $1 billion a year.

Assuming Sex Clubs (Topless and Nude Gentlemen's Clubs) generate on average $7,500 per dancer and assuming 2,500 dancers are working each day, then the sex club income is on the order of 365 x 2,500 x $7,500 = $6,743,800,000 a year, or roughly $7 billion a year.

The total sex industry is generating revenues on the order of $8 billion to probably $10 billion a year.

HOW MUCH DO THE GIRLS MAKE?

A club dancer may pull in $5,000 to $10,000 a night in sales and make 20% in tips for $1,000 to $2,000 per night. If she works five nights a week, she earns $15,000 a week. If she works 40 weeks a year, she pulls in $600,000 a year. Perhaps $100K to $200K is unreported cash income.

PEOPLE that work with pimps, many of who are underage and fall under the sex trafficking laws, may not make any money at all. It should be clear why the city is trying to clean up this segment of the industry.

The Economist, one of the most respected magazines, is now indicating that the sex industry is becoming safer, is a mainstream industry, and that governments need to step up to the plate and legalize the oldest profession as discussed in their articles "A personal choice" and "More bang for your buck."

DRUGS REVENUES CALCULATION

Drug usage in the United States, the highest in the world at 2.8%, is estimated to have a market value at nearly $100 billion in 1997 (twice the amount spent on gasoline). Las Vegas, most likely has a higher drug usage rate because of the high availability and high visitor demand for drugs. In 2011, Fuel Freedom estimated American households spent $4,000 on gasoline. There are approximately 120 million households. Let's look at the numbers:

In the USA there are approximately 120,000,000 households x $4,000 for gasoline/household = $480,000,000,000. At twice this, the amount estimated for illicit drugs, $960,000,000,000/313,000,000 population = $3,058 per capita in elicit drug expenditures. The average population of Las Vegas including tourists is 2,405,479. Therefore, the annual drug industry of Las Vegas can be approximated at 2,405,479 x $3,058 = $7,356,673,590 which equates to a $7.35 billion a year industry. If one were to estimate that Las Vegas, the party capital of the United States, easily uses twice the average amount, then the annual revenues might approximate $14 billion.

The United States took the winner position in the Most Drugged-Out Countries list done by the World Health Organization in 2008. It was estimated that 42.4% of the population have used cannabis and 16.2% have used cocaine. Based on numbers supplied in this recent article the calculations below are understated by nearly 25%. Since 1971, the United States has spent $1 trillion on the war on drugs and still has no concrete numbers, publicly available, of the amount of drugs used in this country. One segment of a war effort is to know the numbers. The $55 billion heroin market is not even discussed here. It is amazing that a country can spend so much money to stop something but actually accomplishes the opposite. Cocaine

The Annual Cocaine market in the USA was approximately $70 billion in 2005. At $100/gram, the total consumption is approximately 700 million grams (770 tons or 12.8 – 60 ton truck loads). The population of the USA is 313.9 million. Therefore, the population on average uses approximately 2.23 grams per year.

The United States topped the world chart with the highest annual prevalence of cocaine use as a percentage of the population aged 15 to 64 in the 2006 World Drug Report at 2.8 percent. This age group represents 66.7% of total population in 2012. Population in 2012 was 313 million. Age group 15-64 equals 208,771,000. At 2.8%, that equals 5,845,588 cocaine users.

2.23 grams/user/year = 13,035,661 grams, or 13.035 metric tons per year.

Wikianswer estimates daily cocaine consumption for USA = 1 ton. One ton x 365 days = 365 tons/year x 1 million grams/ metric ton = 365 million grams.

Per capita consumption = 365 million grams/ 313 million people = 1.16 grams per person/year. At $100/gram, per capita usage = $116.

At an average population in Las Vegas of 2,405,479 people x 1.16 grams/person = 2,797,069 grams per year x $100/gram = an annual market of $279,706,860. At the higher estimated consumption of 2.23 grams/user x the Las Vegas population of 2,405,479 = 5,364,241 grams/year x $100/gram equals an annual market of $536,424,115.

Many would say that Las Vegas, the party/drug city of America, most likely has a consumption of at least 5 times the average. Therefore, one can assume thataine market in Las Vegas is approximately $1.39 billion to $2.68 billion.

 NOTE: 1 metric ton = 1 million grams

Marijuana

Annual usage in the United States = 22,000 metric tons = 776,030,000 oz./USA population 313,900,000 = 2.4722 oz./ person/year.

At 28 joints per oz. = 69.222 joints/year/person/365 = 0.189649788 joints/day

At $250/oz./28 = $9/joint.

Las Vegas Population = 2,405,479 (includes tourists) x 0.189649788 joints/day x 365 days per year =166,512,51 Total Joints per year x $9/joint = $1,498,612,626 or approximately $1.5 billion per year.

Again, these numbers are very conservative and with the highly biased party atmosphere, the number might easily be doubled to approximately $3 billion or to 5 times at $7.5 billion.

The 2008-9 Las Vegas GDP was estimated at <u>$97 billion</u>. There is probably another $7.5 to $14 billion of illicit drug activity on top of that, or 7.73% to 14.4%. These numbers might be easily applied to any American city with only a factor of variation. One can easily imagine the magnitude of the total market if all the other illicit drugs were included.

APPENDIX E
ATTORNEYS

TICKETS

So, you got in a bind and were issued a traffic ticket. If you have been following the recommendations of this book and you were as polite as you were when you met your spouse's parents, you will have a ticket that can be easily handled.

Important! A moving violation in Nevada is a misdemeanor criminal offense. Not like an infraction in California. This is a very "Serious" matter. You can go to jail. Not only that, if you skip out and you live in a neighboring state you can be extradited back to Nevada to resolve it. That may mean a few days in the slammer.

You have three choices:

1. Pay the fine via some of the choices available, such as put a check in the mail. In this case, if it is a moving violation, you will have to deal with an insurance premium increase and it goes on your record as a "misdemeanor criminal offense" with the possible requirement of traffic school.

2. You can come back to Nevada, speak to the judge, and negotiate with the district attorney.

3. You can hire an attorney who handles everything. (An excellent option!)

While you are in Las Vegas, you can contact an attorney (see listings in this appendix). In most cases, unless you did something stupid and seriously bad, you will give the ticket to the attorney (make a copy), give him a check to pay for the ticket fine, and pay an additional fee (usually a very minor amount) for the services.

The attorney will take your ticket to the judge, where in most cases, providing yours is not too serious, they will convert it to a non-criminal parking violation. This means it does not go on your record, your insurance doesn't go up, and there is no requirement for traffic school.

A complete list of Las Vegas attorneys is available on-line. Below is a list of attorneys with helpful information on their websites.

CRIMINAL DEFENSE

Disclaimer: *This book, and its author, do not endorse or recommend any of the Attorneys listed below. It is important for you, the reader, to interview and select an attorney who, to you, best suits your needs.*

Potter Law Offices **(702) 997-1774**

"One of the hidden dangers of Las Vegas, a town famous for its myriad spectacles, is the assumption that prostitution is either a legal activity or that there is no penalty for seeking the services of a prostitute. These misconceptions can easily lead to criminal charges. In the second case, the act of seeking the services of a prostitute is called solicitation. In Nevada, this is categorically defined as an attempted crime."

See the Potter Law Offices website for more information, definitions, laws, and service options.

Las Vegas Defense Group **(702) 333-3673**

This group's web page is very informative and is a must-read prior to going to Las Vegas. There is an instructive video by an attorney where he discusses acts of solicitation and how first-time acts can "almost always" be dismissed with only a requirement for a sexual awareness class.

He also provides instructions on how stings are done. This website is very informative with a complete review of the laws, how they apply, and how reductions in sentences are applied.

Brown Law Offices **(702) 405-0505, (888) 654-6340, cell (702) 595-0641**

There is some discussion on the home page about prostitution with excellent links to specific issues you may encounter.

This attorney's web page indicates that it is "not uncommon" for the police to lack sufficient evidence to charge someone for prostitution. They therefore look for other things to charge suspects with—examples are trespassing in casinos after having been told to leave, loitering outside a business for no apparent reason, using a false ID in a casino or bar, providing false information, or refusing to answer a question or being dishonest in any way. All of which can get you into trouble with a misdemeanor offense that carries up to six months in jail and/or up to $1,000 fine.

This law firm also has a very good discussion of Night Club arrests and Pool Party arrests that is worth a few minutes of reading before engaging in these activities.

Law Office of Chip Siegal (702) 430-7531

This attorney's web page is very instructive with lengthy descriptions of laws and the penalties for crimes committed in Las Vegas. It is worthy of a few minutes of your reading time.

Law Office of Joel M. Mann (702) 474-6266

This website has a good definition list such as "Escort Definition" and "Unlicensed Massage in Las Vegas." This is a good website for further legal definitions; it is a "must-read" site.

APPENDIX F
LINKS

The following links are shortened via TinyURL.com for ease of entering into a browser. All links start with http://tinyurl.com/ and are followed by six or seven characters, which are much easier to remember than some the addresses that exceed 100 characters.

Foreword

Preface

How to use this book

websitedown — http://tinyurl.com/c3n36hr

LasVegasInsidersGuide — http://www.LasVegasInsidersGuide.net

http://tinyurl.com/ — http://tinyurl.com

Introduction

The Baddest Females — http://tinyurl.com/krqnq9y

Male Russian Hunk — http://tinyurl.com/llb4zqf

Blond Russian Knockout — http://tinyurl.com/ptq4qca

Bass Pro — http://tinyurl.com/kvucc2p

50 cal. Desert Eagles — http://tinyurl.com/8w8jhb6

The Judge — http://tinyurl.com/mf3kvr

Video — http://tinyurl.com/maguy9k

Expert — http://tinyurl.com/mrxrbxt

Chapter 1 Las Vegas at a Glance

15 of the largest 25 hotels in the world — http://tinyurl.com/5uxnlk

Crime Map — http://tinyurl.com/okhj5d2

Ask Siri

Smart Phone Apps

App Crawler — http://tinyurl.com/n2g7unt

Where are you?

The Big Sucking Sound

Hotels

Rate Las Vegas — http://tinyurl.com/pbxnvph

Vegas Today and Tomorrow — http://tinyurl.com/3upel6r

South Point — http://tinyurl.com/kzwrktz

M Resort — http://tinyurl.com/ocouu6

Green Valley Ranch — http://tinyurl.com/kyeutw6

Red Rock Casino Resort and Spa — http://tinyurl.com/ld5dwgx

Station Casinos — http://tinyurl.com/k4rxdoc

McCarran International Airport — https://www.mccarran.com/

Vegas.com mobile app — http://tinyurl.com/ngq4eqf

Top 11 Email Services - http://tinyurl.com/2xw74d

Temporary Email Address

Temporary Telephones

Tourism and Conventions

Las Vegas Tourism — http://tinyurl.com/3smwqc4

Convention Calendar — http://tinyurl.com/ljm48l

Vegas Means Business — http://tinyurl.com/l853xy

Map Explorer — http://tinyurl.com/lowuk4f

Surveillance Cameras

What Happens In Vegas Doesn't Stay In Vegas — http://tinyurl.com/k4qvko7

Intellistreets — http://intellistreets.com/

Appearance

Sagging crop — http://tinyurl.com/kjwp96t

Be Polite and Respectful

Tipping

Tipping Guidelines — http://tinyurl.com/ltwalzy

Don't Complain

Las Vegas Trivia

Latter Day Saints — http://tinyurl.com/lnysogj

Getting The Most During Your Stay

Chapter 2 Arriving in Las Vegas

Driving Into Las Vegas

X-Train — http://tinyurl.com/obp3nvn

The Deadliest Stretch of Freeway in America — http://tinyurl.com/okuwska

Interstate 15

Interstate 15 between Los Angeles and Las Vegas — http://tinyurl.com/l23j7vh

Kelso Depot Visitor Center — http://tinyurl.com/osqdnxz

Interstate 15 between Baker and Las Vegas — http://tinyurl.com/kkxgqpp

Interesting Sights

Zzyzx Mineral Springs — http://tinyurl.com/yhwtzj

Molycorp Mine — http://tinyurl.com/mkvkzlx

Bright Source Solar Field — http://tinyurl.com/can9jza

I-15 Tickets – California Highway Patrol (CHP)

Speed Tracker — http://tinyurl.com/o8g5k3g

States Rights — Wonders of the World

The "M" Resort Spa and Casino

Driving In and Around Las Vegas

Segway — http://tinyurl.com/mwexm82

Transportation

Taxi Cabs

Vegas Mate — http://tinyurl.com/ok56h9b

Taxi Fare Finder — http://tinyurl.com/d8q4v7

Example — http://tinyurl.com/knrn8t2

Limousines

Car Rentals

Gas

Gas Buddy — http://tinyurl.com/2wuwu

Buses

Hydrogen-powered buses — http://tinyurl.com/owbjncb

Listing of Transportation Firms — http://tinyurl.com/d9o4lag

Monorail

Las Vegas Monorail — http://tinyurl.com/o2jf8jl

Watch Out For Pedestrians

Traffic Tickets

Fail To Lane Over

Speeding

Cell Phones

Not Using Blinkers

Not Stopping For Pedestrians in Crosswalks

Tickets in Work Zone

Chapter 3 Where Are You

Useful Maps

Interactive Map of Las Vegas — http://tinyurl.com/bomgcc9

General Boundaries Map — http://tinyurl.com/l5dd5et

Interactive Map — http://tinyurl.com/7jk62m6

Gaia GPS — http://tinyurl.com/lsffpaz

Vegas Indoor Maps — http://tinyurl.com/nor98bm

Cardinal Directions

Digital Compass — http://tinyurl.com/kmhogp6

Open Alcoholic Containers

Open Alcoholic Beverage — http://tinyurl.com/ofr2u6s

No Longer Allowed — http://tinyurl.com/onyfcvx

Las Vegas Advisor — http://tinyurl.com/mm77wcu

Flamingo Triangle — http://tinyurl.com/ost4yht

Wise Laws — http://tinyurl.com/k6ew6zk

Massage Parlors

89104 — http://tinyurl.com/n2gml59

Spas

Rub Maps — http://tinyurl.com/3lrakew

Guns

Chapter 4 Crime In Las Vegas

Crime Map — http://tinyurl.com/okhj5d2

Crime In Las Vegas — http://tinyurl.com/o2o8zz6

Deadly Force Exposes the High Risk Zip Codes

Las Vegas Police Rank High In Shootings — http://tinyurl.com/p2c3rp6

89101 — http://tinyurl.com/ow9p9mb

89103 — http://tinyurl.com/mmla4n4

89104 — http://tinyurl.com/nb78ene

89108 — http://tinyurl.com/mlds673

89110 — http://tinyurl.com/morubf3

89115 — http://tinyurl.com/kmu22vp

89121 — http://tinyurl.com/lbod6xp

Crime in Las Vegas - http://tinyurl.com/o2o8zz6

89109 — http://tinyurl.com/lefu9rg

Safety rules-of-thumb

Freemont Street

The Freemont Experience — http://tinyurl.com/k52z986

Chapter 5 Have Fun and Stay Out of Trouble

10 Surest Ways To Get Arrested In Las Vegas — http://tinyurl.com/or7qrva

Card Counting App — http://tinyurl.com/oj7mngj

Common Misdemeanor Charges in Las Vegas

Attorneys

Sex and Politics of Nevada

Brothels — http://tinyurl.com/o4h74

Secret Brothels — http://tinyurl.com/m3p52or

The Legal City

Back Page — http://tinyurl.com/oz679v5

Sex Trafficking

Assembly Bill-AB67 — http://tinyurl.com/kl2rrnc

Signed by Governor — http://tinyurl.com/pwrchrg

Drawing The Line On Sex Trafficking — http://tinyurl.com/pp585xs

How Big Are The Numbers?

Gambling

Casino Markers

Minors

Frequently Asked Questions — http://tinyurl.com/yns3hx

Age of Consent

Dude, she can't even get a driver's license — http://tinyurl.com/bl4ro7p

Nevada Statutory Seduction Law Explained — http://tinyurl.com/c8kyen2

Escort Services — http://tinyurl.com/pghbhqk

Age of Consent — http://tinyurl.com/kj4xhx8

Guns – Concealed Carry

Nevada Department of Public Safety's — http://tinyurl.com/lpgjo47

CCW permits in Nevada — http://tinyurl.com/at6fvwo

Non-Resident CCW — http://tinyurl.com/mgbkntr

Handgunlaw.us — http://tinyurl.com/2bfqn5

CCW Permits and Hotels

Drugs

Crime Map — http://tinyurl.com/okhj5d2

Drug Dictionary — http://tinyurl.com/3s4a7z9

Drug Trafficking — http://tinyurl.com/ksnonhd

Finding an Attorney

List of Las Vegas Attorneys — http://tinyurl.com/ntmd8gt

Potter Law Offices — http://tinyurl.com/7acax2h

Brown Law Offices — http://tinyurl.com/nrc4ece

Law Office of Chip Siegel — http://tinyurl.com/kxexeag

Law Office of Joel M. Mann — http://tinyurl.com/paqxzwr

Chapter 6 Entertainment Clubs

Whats-On — http://tinyurl.com/lrav9wg

Las Vegas Weekly — http://tinyurl.com/km7kvyd

Las Vegas Magazine — http://tinyurl.com/4zz69mv

Seven Magazine — http://tinyurl.com/kg87u4t

Inside Henderson Magazine — http://tinyurl.com/nxqvjy6

Las Vegas Advisor — http://tinyurl.com/5w3ex

Entertainment Clubs

Entertainment Clubs — http://tinyurl.com/gl4z7

Hakkasan Club — http://tinyurl.com/ows8ydq

Light Nightclub — http://tinyurl.com/ludupzr

Entertainment Clubs — http://tinyurl.com/gl4z7

Club Reviews

Yelp's Strip Club Las Vegas — http://tinyurl.com/qdkftja

Bachelor Vegas — http://tinyurl.com/6ssmh58

Naughty Reviews — http://tinyurl.com/muwvbpd

Vegas Travel Site — http://tinyurl.com/gl4z7

Galavantier Las Vegas — http://tinyurl.com/ozuu8nn

Light Night Club — http://tinyurl.com/ludupzr

Surrender Nightclub (89) — http://tinyurl.com/q9pxuk6

Tryst Nightclub (92) — http://tinyurl.com/ld39dts

XS Nightclub (94) — http://tinyurl.com/asdoh2d

Body English (80) — http://tinyurl.com/d7t56u

VIP Club Crawl (90) — http://tinyurl.com/8xtl6qo

Negative Reviews Sapphire - http://tinyurl.com/ccc9q55

Strip Club Etiquette

Strip Club Etiquette — http://tinyurl.com/mv259vw

Funny Money

ATM Machines

Gentlemen's Clubs and Clubs for Women

Club Viva Las Vegas — http://tinyurl.com/6vgqkyo

Topless Clubs or Strip Clubs

Spearmint Rhino — http://tinyurl.com/cvelgj

Special Packages — http://tinyurl.com/a4e3gdf

Cheetahs — http://tinyurl.com/c7p74u5

Club Paradise — http://tinyurl.com/kdndevz

Olympic Garden OC Gentlemen's Club — http://tinyurl.com/knjk3fx

Reviews — http://tinyurl.com/n6wyd3m

Nude Clubs

Little Darlings — http://tinyurl.com/3od5o6f

The Wizard of Vegas — http://tinyurl.com/my8wwu7

Ladies Clubs

Sapphire Gentlemen's Club — http://tinyurl.com/2wtjv

Bachelor Party — http://tinyurl.com/o8w8kv9

Men of Sapphire — http://tinyurl.com/kc8rwzf

Bachelorette Party — http://tinyurl.com/72dlohm

Chippendales The Show — http://tinyurl.com/lxw9oew

Voodoo Steak And Rooftop Night Club — http://tinyurl.com/akxh56h

Thunder From Down Under — http://tinyurl.com/m67t

Pool Parties

Adult and topless pools continue to make waves — http://tinyurl.com/l5yptns

Azure Pool Lounge — http://tinyurl.com/kow9a3a

Tao Beach — http://tinyurl.com/lagrzsk

Bare Pool Lounge — http://tinyurl.com/bt2uocu

Daylight Beach Club — http://tinyurl.com/q7l6uqg

Pool Clubs

The Topless in Las Vegas — http://tinyurl.com/ddnphy

Cool Pools — http://tinyurl.com/rb96z5

Meetup — http://tinyurl.com/lpw7ddl

Sex In Clubs

American Express "Black" Centurion Credit Card — http://tinyurl.com/6z9ebrk

Gay Clubs and Bars

Las Vegas GLBT bars, clubs, and pool clubs — http://tinyurl.com/e4vs5

LV Gay Bar Guide - Best Gay Nightlife in LV — http://tinyurl.com/nsvphoo

900 Block of E. Sahara — http://tinyurl.com/ohycaok

Crime Map — http://tinyurl.com/okhj5d2

The Garage — http://tinyurl.com/apuludc

Drink and Drag — http://www.drinkanddrag.com/

Snicks Place — http://tinyurl.com/pd3jnzt

Share — http://tinyurl.com/mgocu9y

Piranha — http://tinyurl.com/85ykw79

Bars — http://tinyurl.com/l7xcsyd

Complete Planning Tools — http://tinyurl.com/qejw6ud

Chapter 7 VIP Services

SheetsVIP — http://tinyurl.com/n6yxrml

Galavantier — http://tinyurl.com/ozuu8nn

Club Viva Las Vegas — http://tinyurl.com/6vgqkyo

Red Carpet VIP — http://tinyurl.com/lqg8ytv

Vegas VIP — http://tinyurl.com/7le5uve

Vegas Inside Players — http://tinyurl.com/l87lhhp

Chapter 8 Gambling

Gambling Plan

Feeling Good About Yourself

The Wizard of Odds — http://tinyurl.com/7xjkw4x

The Wizard of Vegas — http://tinyurl.com/cedvf3z

The Ten Commandments of Gambling — http://tinyurl.com/mzpwesp

Casino Guide — http://tinyurl.com/ylsaejo

Chapter 9 Sex in Las Vegas

Legal Reminders

  Las Vegas crime map — http://tinyurl.com/okhj5d2

  10 Girls to Avoid in Las Vegas — http://tinyurl.com/8u5w74r

  RICO — http://tinyurl.com/f3jux

  Sex Industry Put On Notice — http://tinyurl.com/l5l6b9r

Hotels

Web Cams

  Ten indispensible technologies — http://tinyurl.com/lja85mv

  Porn: The Hidden Engine — http://tinyurl.com/k6ynyt4

  Live Web Cams — http://tinyurl.com/ko7rhbw

Escorts Out-call and In-call

  Naughty Reviews (escorts)(female) — http://tinyurl.com/
    lefw4jr

  Naughty Reviews (escorts)(male) — http://tinyurl.com/ksus9k5

  Naughty Reviews — http://tinyurl.com/ks78y3y

Female Escorts

Escort Agencies

Shemale Escorts

Male Escorts for Ladies

  Cowboys 4 Angels — http://tinyurl.com/q46w6km

  Cougars — http://tinyurl.com/yspaw2

  Cowboy — http://tinyurl.com/pv2c44u

  Cowboys 4 Angels — http://tinyurl.com/q46w6km

Street Cards

  Prostitution in Las Vegas — http://tinyurl.com/ybg4uk2

Chinese Newspapers

Escorts and Massage Independents

  Eros Guide Las Vegas — http://tinyurl.com/n4t6ttc

  City Vibe — http://tinyurl.com/nx7lu4d

  Blond Russian Knockout — http://tinyurl.com/ptq4qca

Personal website — http://tinyurl.com/yb6bjjd

Adultfax Review — http://tinyurl.com/m2wgyrw

LVFever — http://tinyurl.com/mqkha8d

The Erotic Review — http://tinyurl.com/m48avho

Available Escort — http://tinyurl.com/pudhqy

Her personal web page — http://tinyurl.com/mgekzpy

Las Vegas Escort Prices — http://tinyurl.com/q3bxce2

Limousine Services

Las Vegas Limo Diaries — http://tinyurl.com/mukoqnr

One More Sin Escorts — http://tinyurl.com/ke393l6

Brothel Options — http://tinyurl.com/jvqmg7j

Personals

Craigslist — http://tinyurl.com/887ql

Therapeutic Services — http://tinyurl.com/n938u5m

Back Page — http://tinyurl.com/6pjz6ee

Female Escorts — http://tinyurl.com/k549nt6

Male Escorts — http://tinyurl.com/ly6hvg8

Male Russian Hunk — http://tinyurl.com/llb4zqf

His web page — http://tinyurl.com/k9wqmta

Massage Parlors and Spas

Imperial Health Spa — http://tinyurl.com/kmyc52e

Rubmaps — http://tinyurl.com/3lrakew

Finding Your Massage Parlor

Rubmaps — http://tinyurl.com/3lrakew

Slang Tab — http://tinyurl.com/kj7mbzj

Erotic MP — http://tinyurl.com/2crqvjf

Adult Search Erotic Massage — http://tinyurl.com/lymqqxk

Naughty Reviews — http://tinyurl.com/kav4qn2

Massage Exchange — http://tinyurl.com/mpwc6c7

Vegas Spa Guide For Men — http://tinyurl.com/jwfge3h

Masseur Finder — http://tinyurl.com/lbj4heu

Eros Guide to Massage Las Vegas — http://tinyurl.com/n4t6ttc

Street Hookers

Crime Map — http://tinyurl.com/okhj5d2

Working Girls — http://tinyurl.com/mgorv8c

Swingers Clubs

Las Vegas Red Rooster — http://tinyurl.com/28le8d3

The Fantasy Swingers Club — http://tinyurl.com/3bbmb4c

Swingers Circle — http://tinyurl.com/p5jgghw

The Green Door — http://tinyurl.com/mv5owdd

Green Door Yelp review — http://tinyurl.com/ndu2jps

SDC.com — http://tinyurl.com/n67wvw7

Gay Activities

Bluemoon — http://tinyurl.com/3gfzfh

Bluemoon Yelp Reviews — http://tinyurl.com/n5exl58

Rentboy — http://tinyurl.com/n4gtaxq

Men4rentnow — http://tinyurl.com/4qzom2

Rentmen — http://tinyurl.com/ov3f8yo

Squirt — http://tinyurl.com/2ws3z

Hawks Gym — http://tinyurl.com/kw5pmr9

Entourage Vegas Spa & Health Club — http://tinyurl.com/mbm47zo

Imperial Health Spa — http://tinyurl.com/mr8e2w3

Imperial Health Spa Services — http://tinyurl.com/kmyc52e

Good Reviews — http://tinyurl.com/muxs9or

Groupon Spa Pass — http://tinyurl.com/ltf6b6k

Chapter 10 Legal Prostitution - Brothels

Prostitution is legal — http://tinyurl.com/o4h74

Prostitution — http://tinyurl.com/ybg4uk2

28 Operating Brothels — http://tinyurl.com/6cumea

Sheri's Ranch — http://tinyurl.com/c6mmn

Chicken Ranch — http://tinyurl.com/32o6ca

Sheri's Ranch — http://tinyurl.com/c6mmn

Line Up — http://tinyurl.com/m27ry3m

Sex Menu — http://tinyurl.com/3qusgr4

Themed Bungalow Suites — http://tinyurl.com/llb4s8n

Hi End Lady — http://tinyurl.com/l4e7e5j

Chicken Ranch — http://tinyurl.com/32o6ca

Petite Young Hottie — http://tinyurl.com/kzfnag6

History — http://tinyurl.com/kr3wygh

Shady Lady Ranch — http://tinyurl.com/lfzjch

Love Ranch Southern NV — http://tinyurl.com/ahdtlps

Chapter 11 Drugs

4th ranked state for prescription drug overdose… — http://tinyurl.com/mtx2awl

Las Vegas ranking second — http://tinyurl.com/qcoj7gc

46,052 combined drug users in Las Vegas — http://tinyurl.com/lsvsaxu

Las Vegas Wal-Mart — http://tinyurl.com/ml73hrj

Methamphetamine use at epidemic proportions — http://tinyurl.com/lo7owkk

Huge population trend — http://tinyurl.com/e9fcg

22 million illegal drug users — http://tinyurl.com/6fzdlw2

How to Score Weed in Las Vegas — http://tinyurl.com/kqoa2cm

Price of Weed — http://tinyurl.com/n6nkllq

Ecstasy — http://tinyurl.com/72p55ak

Cocaine — http://tinyurl.com/lgqmm45

Methamphetamine — http://tinyurl.com/p2t2w97

GHB — http://tinyurl.com/7um65dl

Heroin — http://tinyurl.com/y7adzn

Former Prosecutor's Website — http://tinyurl.com/ksnonhd

Defenses — http://tinyurl.com/k4uw8k2

The Underground FDA

Dance Safe — http://tinyurl.com/84u89

Dance Safe Test Kit — http://tinyurl.com/kr47of9

Drug Aid — http://tinyurl.com/n23g3g3

Detox Answers — http://tinyurl.com/m7eewre

Moon Rocks: The Best High On Earth — http://tinyurl.com/b54fog2

Ecstasydata.org — http://tinyurl.com/ncb33

Chapter 12 - Guns

Tenth Amendment to the Constitution — http://tinyurl.com/by47x

Concealed Carry

Concealed Firearm Permits — http://tinyurl.com/at6fvwo

Nevada Concealed Carry — http://tinyurl.com/pqh4mwc

Department of Public Safety — http://tinyurl.com/lpgjo47

Firearms Training

5 Arrows Tactical Training — http://tinyurl.com/pr7slsc

Las Vegas Firearms Training — http://tinyurl.com/keg4h4y

Front Sight Firearms Training Institute — http://tinyurl.com/3ypy7z

Desert Shooting

BLM Southern Nevada District Office — http://tinyurl.com/7u5sbcd

Las Vegas Interactive Map — http://tinyurl.com/kyyw3g3

Las Vegas Valley Target Shooting Closure Map — http://tinyurl.com/kklqtfh

Pahrump Closure Map — http://tinyurl.com/l3qdo3z

Firearms Shipping

Davidson Firearms — http://tinyurl.com/lqmbwem

Shooting Ranges

The Range 702 — http://tinyurl.com/qhqbnve

The Gun Store — http://tinyurl.com/3uylrcf

Machine Guns Vegas — http://tinyurl.com/6wwqr8f

Battlefield Vegas — http://tinyurl.com/mw7vyet

Trip Advisor — http://tinyurl.com/br27ewq

Battlefield Vegas — http://tinyurl.com/mw7vyet

Pro Gun Club — http://tinyurl.com/pwhvvhr

Sure Fire Institute — http://tinyurl.com/jvjck3c

Blow Sh!t Up — http://tinyurl.com/kq8a2d5

E-ticket — http://tinyurl.com/my5uk

Great Reviews — http://tinyurl.com/p9e6a8c

Pro Gun Club — http://tinyurl.com/pwhvvhr

Clark County Shooting Complex — http://tinyurl.com/ksmxxdy

Clark County Shooting Complex review — http://tinyurl.com/kf2raoz

Clark County Shooting Complex — http://tinyurl.com/ksmxxdy

Chapter 13 Preferred Cards, Buffets, and Restaurants

Preferred Cards

YELP — http://tinyurl.com/kzau34v

Coupon Grabber — http://tinyurl.com/kgoq4yp

Tix4tonight — http://tinyurl.com/d8kfpzj

Buffets

Best Buffets in Las Vegas — http://tinyurl.com/n4gbf3c

Ten Best Las Vegas Buffets…All You Can Eat… — http://tinyurl.com/lvppoa2

Vegas Buffets: Five to Find — http://tinyurl.com/lhwh48h

Best Buffets in Las Vegas — http://tinyurl.com/7vm5wz7

24 Hour Buffet Pass — http://tinyurl.com/lpko6mu

Jules Monty — http://tinyurl.com/lrc6pst

The Feast Buffet — http://tinyurl.com/qctzz76

Green Valley Ranch Resort — http://tinyurl.com/kyeutw6

Green Valley Ranch Resort — http://tinyurl.com/kyeutw6

Festival Buffet — http://tinyurl.com/ppdtsm6

Fiesta Hotel in Henderson — http://tinyurl.com/oeu7xjm

Fiesta Hotel in Henderson — http://tinyurl.com/oeu7xjm

Studio B Buffet — http://tinyurl.com/2ex4zqq

M Resort Spa Casino — http://tinyurl.com/ocouu6

M Resort Spa Casino — http://tinyurl.com/ocouu6

Village Seafood Buffet — http://tinyurl.com/nv3ds53

Rio Las Vegas — http://tinyurl.com/ma8huba

Rio Las Vegas — http://tinyurl.com/ma8huba

Bistro Buffet — http://tinyurl.com/mm8nwub

Best Cheap Buffet in Las Vegas — http://tinyurl.com/l7xonx9

The Palms Casino Resort — http://tinyurl.com/e6l9g

The Buffet — http://tinyurl.com/kjfjy9y

Wynn Las Vegas and Encore Hotel — http://tinyurl.com/ltut2dg

Excellent Restaurants

Trip Advisor — http://tinyurl.com/cjzzu2e

Tix4Tonight — http://tinyurl.com/d8kfpzj

Rao's Las Vegas — http://tinyurl.com/lpzjk54

Rao's Reviews — http://tinyurl.com/khufzvh

Rao's Las Vegas — http://tinyurl.com/lpzjk54

Hugo's Cellar — http://tinyurl.com/kbw3oec

Hugo's Reviews — http://tinyurl.com/njw57so

Fremont Experience — http://tinyurl.com/8npee

Hugo's Cellar — http://tinyurl.com/kbw3oec

Tom Collicchio's Craftsteak — http://tinyurl.com/2e5apw3

Tom Collicchio's Reviews - http://tinyurl.com/pdhatpj

Tom Collicchio's Craftsteak — http://tinyurl.com/2e5apw3

Del Frisco's Double Eagle Stake House — http://tinyurl.com/k2dbnhu

Del Frisco's Reviews — http://tinyurl.com/nx7k85l

Del Frisco's Double Eagle Stake House — http://tinyurl.com/k2dbnhu

The Eiffel Tower Restaurant — http://tinyurl.com/bl6dwv

The Eiffel Tower Restaurant Reviews — http://tinyurl.com/mm4jd22

The Eiffel Tower Restaurant — http://tinyurl.com/bl6dwv

Lawry's The Prime Rib Steakhouse — http://tinyurl.com/d2kvfrn

Lawry's The Prime Rib Steakhouse reviews — http://tinyurl.com/oys7lzh

Lawry's The Prime Rib — http://tinyurl.com/d2kvfrn

Soho Japanese Restaurant - http://tinyurl.com/7k7omff

Soho Japanese Restaurant reviews — http://tinyurl.com/lfczd4n

Soho Japanese Restaurant — http://tinyurl.com/7k7omff

The Landings HND Restaurant — http://tinyurl.com/mkkehxn

The Landings HND Restaurant reviews — http://tinyurl.com/o58xxsj

Trip Advisor — http://tinyurl.com/mlevmlh
The Landings HND Restaurant — http://tinyurl.com/mkkehxn
Top of the World Restaurant — http://tinyurl.com/mrq2jdf
Top of the World reviews — http://tinyurl.com/7nlznm8
Vegas.com — http://tinyurl.com/bm84d9u
Top of the World Stratosphere — http://tinyurl.com/m59a6zm
Lotus of Siam — http://tinyurl.com/m9jyk5u
Trip Advisor — http://tinyurl.com/qhfl6lo
Good Reviews — http://tinyurl.com/lkkyzku
Lotus of Siam — http://tinyurl.com/m9jyk5u
Best Pizza in Las Vegas — http://tinyurl.com/m5fs7j2
Best Burgers in Las Vegas — http://tinyurl.com/kjr8bsh
Bachi Burgers — http://tinyurl.com/3x6sd7f

Chapter 14 Entertainment

Cirque du Soleil — http://tinyurl.com/p6m6vg8
Tix4tonight — http://tinyurl.com/lk66rkg
Tix4tonight for locations — http://tinyurl.com/6zxyhk
Tix4tonight location map — http://tinyurl.com/mtlgduh
Best of Vegas — http://tinyurl.com/85t4ujj
Best of Vegas — http://tinyurl.com/85t4ujj
SmarterVegas — http://www.smartervegas.com/
Vegas.com — http://tinyurl.com/pa3ry
Show tickets.com — http://tinyurl.com/n24tvwr

Cirque du Soleil Shows

Love - The Beatles — http://tinyurl.com/p6m6vg8
Mirage Las Vegas — http://tinyurl.com/fdwam
Vegas.com — http://www.vegas.com/shows/
Zumanity — http://tinyurl.com/p6m6vg8
New York New York — http://tinyurl.com/3sbqof7
Vegas.com — http://www.vegas.com/shows/
Mystère — http://tinyurl.com/p6m6vg8
Treasure Island — http://tinyurl.com/kz639za
Vegas.com — http://www.vegas.com/shows/

Criss Angel Believe — http://tinyurl.com/p6m6vg8

Luxor — http://tinyurl.com/4v7pe

Vegas.com — http://www.vegas.com/shows/

O — http://tinyurl.com/p6m6vg8

Bellagio Las Vegas — http://tinyurl.com/d34j5

Vegas.com — http://www.vegas.com/shows/

KÀ — http://tinyurl.com/p6m6vg8

MGM Grand — http://tinyurl.com/zwjup

Vegas.com — http://www.vegas.com/shows/

Zarkana — http://tinyurl.com/p6m6vg8

Aria Resort & Casino — http://tinyurl.com/m7ca3s2

Vegas.com — http://www.vegas.com/shows/

Michael Jackson ONE — http://tinyurl.com/p6m6vg8

Mandalay Bay — http://tinyurl.com/fx9w4

Vegas.com — http://www.vegas.com/shows/

Entertainment Shows

Show Tickets.com — http://tinyurl.com/n24tvwr

Adult Shows

Adult Shows — http://tinyurl.com/l3kzkv3

Thunder Down Under — http://tinyurl.com/mwnk7ft

Excalibur Hotel Casino — http://tinyurl.com/kovmr

Chippendales — http://tinyurl.com/mfcbzuu

Rio Las Vegas — http://tinyurl.com/m6uemac

Absinthe — http://tinyurl.com/lpjakd8

Caesars Palace Las Vegas — http://tinyurl.com/e9d5z

Jubilee — http://tinyurl.com/ksd9ddk

Bally's Casino Las Vegas — http://tinyurl.com/kd32oxm

X Rocks — http://tinyurl.com/mqzu4a6

Rio Las Vegas — http://tinyurl.com/m6uemac

X Burlesque — http://tinyurl.com/lah9rlb

Flamingo Las Vegas — http://tinyurl.com/lxt45

Night School 4 Girls — http://tinyurl.com/l7kcx6z

Hard Rock Café Las Vegas — http://tinyurl.com/hobqk

Pin Up — http://tinyurl.com/lvd9uln
Stratosphere — http://tinyurl.com/nnsqxhl

Broadway/Theater

Broadway/Theater — http://tinyurl.com/lbqaxhd
Rock of Ages - http://tinyurl.com/p4agwqh
Venetian - http://tinyurl.com/pqfobaj
Blue Man Group - http://tinyurl.com/lkrjrgx
Monte Carlo LV Resort & Casino - http://tinyurl.com/zzxg8
Le Rêve - http://tinyurl.com/q59ekz6
Wynn Las Vegas — http://tinyurl.com/b3qao2
Jersey Boys - http://tinyurl.com/nuyvvsz
Paris LV Hotel & Casino - http://tinyurl.com/ofxker8
Dancing Queen - http://tinyurl.com/pvz7prt
Planet Hollywood Resort — http://tinyurl.com/d8kxhj
Vegas the Show - http://tinyurl.com/nq6ovz2
Planet Hollywood Resort - http://tinyurl.com/d8kxhj
Jabbawockeez - http://tinyurl.com/mr7n3b5
Monte Carlo LV Resort & Casino - http://tinyurl.com/zzxg8
Menopause the Musical - http://tinyurl.com/m4827z5
Luxor Las Vegas - http://tinyurl.com/4v7pe
Million Dollar Quartet - http://tinyurl.com/qdf5qyc
Harrah's Las Vegas — http://tinyurl.com/capwhsl

Magic and Hypnosis

Magic and Hypnosis Shows — http://tinyurl.com/nsbwkfj
David Copperfield — http://tinyurl.com/qbvuukx
MGM Grand — http://tinyurl.com/zwjup

Well Known Stars

Caesars Palace — http://tinyurl.com/lux8xa5
Mirage Las Vegas — http://tinyurl.com/zrj7r
Jay Leno — http://tinyurl.com/6lon6nb
Rodney Carrington — http://tinyurl.com/mc2fz2d
MGM Grand Entertainment Calendar — http://tinyurl.com/gq8jm

Chapter 15 Adrenaline Rush

Sky Combat Ace (SCA) — http://tinyurl.com/kqs46ez

Sky Jump — http://tinyurl.com/2dlv3py

Stratosphere — http://tinyurl.com/2g5eod5

Vegas Indoor Skydiving — http://tinyurl.com/l65zsd

Dream Racing — http://tinyurl.com/kxetedq

Richard Petty Driving Experience — http://tinyurl.com/l5vspas

Exotics Racing — http://tinyurl.com/klfc8x8

14 exotic cars — http://tinyurl.com/n7ndjq5\

Dig This — http://tinyurl.com/d6yhjhw

VORE -Vegas Off Road Experience — http://tinyurl.com/
m49j3ed

Chapter 16 Photography

Sol: Sun Clock — http://tinyurl.com/n9mmd5m

Sun Surveyor Lite — http://tinyurl.com/kehl9t6

Stratosphere Tower — http://tinyurl.com/cezhuuy

Top of the World — http://tinyurl.com/mrq2jdf

Foundation Room — http://tinyurl.com/lqz694w

Mix Lounge — http://tinyurl.com/8y2os6s

Voodoo Rooftop Nightclub — http://tinyurl.com/lzr8rtz

Terminal 1Short Term Parking Structure — http://tinyurl.com/
mtnvf3p

High Roller — http://tinyurl.com/n9y326g

Chapter 17 Some Fun Things To Do

The Landings Restaurant– Henderson Executive Airport

The Landings Restaurant — http://tinyurl.com/mkkehxn

Trip Advisor — http://tinyurl.com/mlevmlh

Yelp — http://tinyurl.com/k9mefnl

Running Tail Numbers

Running Tail Numbers — http://tinyurl.com/qck5wd8

Live Flight Tracking — http://tinyurl.com/myewu7a

Registration History — http://tinyurl.com/oa52oor

Tony Stewart — http://tinyurl.com/m69wb8s

Museums

Museums in Las Vegas — http://tinyurl.com/c39tmzd

National Atomic Test Museum — http://tinyurl.com/7yqe48m

Auto Collections — http://tinyurl.com/oe9obss

The Mob Museum — http://tinyurl.com/c4258ud

Spas

Episage Wellness Center — http://tinyurl.com/lwddf5h

Trip Advisor Reviews — http://tinyurl.com/mxetdfn

Elements Massage Summerlin — http://tinyurl.com/o2znkdg

Elements Massage Henderson — http://tinyurl.com/n88m7qm

My Spa — http://tinyurl.com/prn34l5

Encore Spa at the Wynn — http://tinyurl.com/6rdm5pv

Trip Advisor Reviews — http://tinyurl.com/qyozbfl

Qua Baths and Spa — http://tinyurl.com/lvq89nq

Reviews — http://tinyurl.com/p4d8eb9

Boracay — http://tinyurl.com/k6j2fnv

Excellent Reviews — http://tinyurl.com/paklbz3

Gyms

Las Vegas Athletic Clubs — http://tinyurl.com/ljrf3up

The High Roller

High Roller — http://tinyurl.com/n9y326g

LINQ - http://tinyurl.com/lgckyh5

Observation Wheel — http://tinyurl.com/pu79ejk

Tickets — http://tinyurl.com/lgckyh5

Grand Canyon Tours

Maverick Aviation Group — http://tinyurl.com/psqfdp6

Chapter 18 Marriage and Divorce

Marriage

Las Vegas Weddings — http://tinyurl.com/869ds9h

Marriage Requirements — http://tinyurl.com/oqvytaj

Clark County Requirements — http://tinyurl.com/3nc7znk

On-line Pre-marriage Application — http://tinyurl.
com/83aw45w

Nevada Revised Statutes for Marriage — http://tinyurl.com/
lkcpkf3

Vegas.com — http://tinyurl.com/jwg9nyg

Divorce

Divorces in Nevada — http://tinyurl.com/kneqlok

Complete your Nevada divorce online — http://tinyurl.com/
nyenh6w

Nevada Revised Statutes for Divorce — http://tinyurl.
com/882r34z

Chapter 19 Leaving in Style

Lucky Jets — http://tinyurl.com/mmqfjhj

Las Vegas VIP Entertainment Guide — http://tinyurl.
com/7rqrz89

Cirrus Aviation — http://tinyurl.com/lyafplf

NV Jets — http://tinyurl.com/6ue5ddp

Appendix A – Maps

Las Vegas Metropolitan Area

Las Vegas Metropolitan Area information — http://tinyurl.
com/yd6xv52

Boundaries Map — http://tinyurl.com/l5dd5et

Las Vegas Metro Area Map — http://tinyurl.com/mucduo9

Interactive Map of Las Vegas — http://tinyurl.com/bomgcc9

Strip — http://tinyurl.com/kw3pk7y

City of Las Vegas

City of Las Vegas — http://tinyurl.com/ljqm2

Interactive Map — http://tinyurl.com/7jk62m6

Clark County

Clark County — http://tinyurl.com/agxxqyq

Metropolitan area of Las Vegas — http://tinyurl.com/l5rdhwy

Clark County maps section — http://tinyurl.com/7fndcz6

North Las Vegas — http://tinyurl.com/6zazms

Paradise — http://tinyurl.com/d2k3jl

Enterprise — http://tinyurl.com/lzdoopf

Spring Valley — http://tinyurl.com/lztwtml

Sunrise Manor — http://tinyurl.com/kheyjgl

Winchester — http://tinyurl.com/l9eedne

City of Henderson

City of Henderson — http://tinyurl.com/43vmon3

Henderson City Limits Maps — http://tinyurl.com/nfaa4yb

GIS — http://tinyurl.com/7p85axr

Boulder City

Boulder City — http://tinyurl.com/lxztww8

Boulder City Maps Website — http://tinyurl.com/k8b8c3e

Appendix B — Laws and Ordinances

NOTE — Full URL addresses are used for Nevada Revised Statutes (NRS) because TinyURL's do not work well on the Nevada database.

State of Nevada

State of Nevada Revised Statutes — http://www.leg.state.nv.us/Nrs/

Section 200.364 — Sexual Assault and Seduction: Definitions — http://www.leg.state.nv.us/Nrs/NRS-200.html

NRS 200.364 — http://www.leg.state.nv.us/Nrs/NRS-200.html

NRS 200.3784 — http://www.leg.state.nv.us/Nrs/NRS-200.html

NRS 201.540 — http://www.leg.state.nv.us/Nrs/NRS-201.html

NRS 201.550 — http://www.leg.state.nv.us/Nrs/NRS-201.html

NRS 201.300 — http://www.leg.state.nv.us/Nrs/NRS-201.html

NRS 200.366 — http://www.leg.state.nv.us/Nrs/NRS-200.html

NRS 200.368 — http://www.leg.state.nv.us/Nrs/NRS-200.html

NRS Section 200.366 — **Sexual Assault: Definition; penalties** — http://www.leg.state.nv.us/Nrs/NRS-200.html

NRS 201.180 — http://www.leg.state.nv.us/Nrs/NRS-201.html

NRS 201.230 — http://www.leg.state.nv.us/Nrs/NRS-201.html

NRS 201.262 – http://www.leg.state.nv.us/Nrs/NRS-201.html

NRS 201.560 – http://www.leg.state.nv.us/Nrs/NRS-201.html

NRS 201.210 – **Open or Gross Lewdness** –
http://www.leg.state.nv.us/Nrs/NRS-201.html

NRS 193.130 – http://www.leg.state.nv.us/Nrs/NRS-193.html

NRS 193.130 – **Categories and punishment of felonies** –
http://www.leg.state.nv.us/Nrs/NRS-193.html

NRS 176A.100 – http://www.leg.state.nv.us/Nrs/NRS-176A.
html

NRS 244.345 – **Dancing halls, escort services, entertainment
by referral services and gambling games or devices;
limitations on licensing of houses of prostitution**
– http://www.leg.state.nv.us/nrs/NRS-244.html

Chapter 364 – http://www.leg.state.nv.us/nrs/NRS-364.html

Chapter 269 – http://www.leg.state.nv.us/nrs/NRS-269.html

NRS 241.0355 – http://www.leg.state.nv.us/nrs/NRS-241.html

NRS Chapter 453 – **Controlled Substances** –
http://www.leg.state.nv.us/nrs/NRS-453.html

NRS 453.043 – **"Controlled Substances Analog" defined.**
http://www.leg.state.nv.us/nrs/NRS-453.html

NRS 453.166 – http://www.leg.state.nv.us/nrs/NRS-453.html

NRS 453.176 – http://www.leg.state.nv.us/nrs/NRS-453.html

NRS 200.471 – Assault – http://www.leg.state.nv.us/nrs/NRS-
200.html

NRS 200.390 – Battery – http://www.leg.state.nv.us/nrs/NRS-
200.html

NRS Chapter 484C – Driving Under The Influence of Alcohol or
Prohibited Substance – http://www.leg.state.nv.us/NRS/
NRS-484C.html

NRS 205.0821 – Petit Theft – http://www.leg.state.nv.us/
NRS/NRS-205.html

NRS 453.336 – Local Drug Possession– http://www.leg.state.
nv.us/NRS/NRS-453.html

NRS 201.354 – Prostitution– http://www.leg.state.nv.us/
NRS/NRS-201.html

NRS 207.200 — Trespassing— http://www.leg.state.nv.us/ NRS/NRS-207.html

NRS Chapter 205 — Vandalism — http://www.leg.state.nv.us/ Nrs/NRS-205.html

NRS 205.0832 — Shoplifting— http://www.leg.state.nv.us/ Nrs/NRS-205.html

NRS 199.280 — Resisting Arrest— http://www.leg.state.nv.us/ NRS/NRS-199.html

NRS 484 — Traffic Tickets— http://www.leg.state.nv.us/NRS/ NRS-484.html

NRS 484B.165 — Driving while Texting, Phoning, or using other Electronic Devices — http://www.leg.state.nv.us/NRS/ NRS-484B.html - NRS484BSec165

Clark County

Clark County Code of Ordinances library — http://tinyurl.com/ ouy7xvf

Chapter 6.140 — Outcall Promoters...En — http://tinyurl.com/ ouy7xvf

Chapter 6.140.140 — Outcall regulations — http://tinyurl.com/ ouy7xvf

Chapter 6.140.150 Prostitution unlawful — http://tinyurl.com/ ouy7xvf

Chapter 7.08 — Massage Industry — http://tinyurl.com/ ouy7xvf

Chapter 7.54 — Sexually Oriented Com Enterprises — http:// tinyurl.com/ouy7xvf

12.04.180 — Concealed weapons prohibited w/o — http:// tinyurl.com/ouy7xvf

Chapter 12.04.200 — Concealed weapons prohibited w/o permit — http://tinyurl.com/ldhkj7y

City of Las Vegas

City of Las Vegas Municipal Codes Library — http://tinyurl. com/lnl8mkp

City of North Las Vegas

City of North Las Vegas Municipal Codes Library — http:// tinyurl.com/llv3spb

Chapter 9.16 — Controlled Substances — http://tinyurl.com/ lpkdkr4

City of Henderson

City of Henderson Municipal Codes Library — http://tinyurl.com/mxy9kou

Section 04.84 — Massage Establishments and — http://tinyurl.com/mxy9kou

Section 04.85 - Reflexology — http://tinyurl.com/75n3ozm

Boulder City

Boulder City Municipal Codes Library — http://tinyurl.com/ny2y3xe

Title 4 Chapter 10 — http://tinyurl.com/ny2y3xe

Appendix C — Guns

NOTE — Full URL addresses are used for Nevada Revised Statutes (NRS) because TinyURL's do not work well on the Nevada database.

Nevada Revised Statutes on Guns

NRS 202.253 — http://www.leg.state.nv.us/NRs/NRS-202.html

NRS 202.3653 — http://www.leg.state.nv.us/NRs/NRS-202.html

NRS 202.320 — http://www.leg.state.nv.us/NRs/NRS-202.html

NRS 202.287 — http://www.leg.state.nv.us/NRs/NRS-202.html

North Las Vegas Gun Laws

Chapter 9.32 — http://tinyurl.com/1pkdkr4

Chapter 9.36 — http://tinyurl.com/1pkdkr4

Clark County Gun Laws

12.04.230 Discharging unlawful—Exceptions — http://tinyurl.com/ouy7xvf

Shooting Closure Areas

Las Vegas Valley Target Shooting Closure Map — http://tinyurl.com/kklqtfh

Pahrump Closure Map — http://tinyurl.com/l3qdo3z

Appendix D – Prostitution and Drug Calculations

Prostitution Calculation

Sex Revenue

Wikipedia — http://tinyurl.com/6jg9bd

Sex Industry and Sex Workers in Nevada — http://tinyurl.com/mbqj3q9

How Much Do Girls Make?

A personal choice — http://tinyurl.com/og2ucwm

More bang for your buck — http://tinyurl.com/k8v5pwh

Drug Revenues Calculation

American ... spent $4,000 on gasoline — http://tinyurl.com/l3pm2l4

Most Drugged-Out Countries — http://tinyurl.com/lkv55ks

Recent Article —http://tinyurl.com/oegnh6e

Cocaine

Annual Cocaine market — http://tinyurl.com/mb9zpa3

2006 World Drug Report — http://tinyurl.com/2u794xa

66.7% of total pop in 2012 — http://tinyurl.com/ko6umsw

Population in 2012 was 313 million — http://tinyurl.com/79ygwoj

Marijuana

22,000 metric tons — http://tinyurl.com/27rtoyb

$97 billion — http://tinyurl.com/md9g83r

Appendix E — Attorneys

Tickets

List of Las Vegas Attorneys — http://tinyurl.com/ntmd8gt

Criminal Defense

Potter Law Offices — http://tinyurl.com/7acax2h

Las Vegas Defense Group — http://tinyurl.com/c3wcshz

Brown Law Offices — http://tinyurl.com/nrc4ece

Law Office of Chip Siegal — http://tinyurl.com/kxexeag

Law Office of Joel M. Mann — http://tinyurl.com/paqxzwr

Appendix F — Links

Appendix G – Smart Phone Apps

Vegasmate – http://tinyurl.com/ok56h9b

Travel Vegas – http://tinyurl.com/pp6kt3g

Vegas Indoor Maps – http://tinyurl.com/nor98bm

Heading Compass – http://tinyurl.com/kmhogp6

Gas Buddy – http://tinyurl.com/p7mjlge

GAIA GPS – http://tinyurl.com/prefy88

Sun Surveyor Lite – http://tinyurl.com/kehl9t6

Sol Sun Clock – http://tinyurl.com/q5jdxtx

Speed Tracker – http://tinyurl.com/o8g5k3g

Vegas – http://tinyurl.com/ngq4eqf

AAA Mobile – http://tinyurl.com/b2jo928

Wish Dates – http://tinyurl.com/p4gqqv2

BreakTheIce – http://tinyurl.com/n8oahpn

OkCupid – http://tinyurl.com/kx89lfp

Skout – http://tinyurl.com/mgcaopl

WhoseHere – http://tinyurl.com/mdfcuas

APPENDIX G
SMART PHONE APPS

A very useful website for finding smart phone apps is <u>AppCrawlr</u>, the App discovery engine. Below are a number of useful apps to save time and money while in Las Vegas.

<u>Vegas Mate</u> — This app has a lot of information in it for the tourist. The most valuable part of this app is the Check Cab at the bottom of Hotels, Dining, Clubs and Pools, Shows, and Activates pages. The Check Cab will show the route and the cost for a cab. If you are close, the app also shows the best route and walk time. The Shows page gives very good cost saving advice on savings for different shows such as the 50% discount code to use when buying a specific ticket on-line. This app also has a very good map/satellite viewer with hotels clearly noted.

<u>Travel Vegas</u> — This app features discounts on many cool things to do, see, eat, and enjoy in Las Vegas. This app includes hand picked discounts (up to 50%) from airline flights, restaurants, and tours. The app specials include: Free drinks, gambling credits, dining discounts, half off show tickets, and more. The app also includes a map that shows hotel locations. Updated daily.

<u>Vegas Indoor Maps</u> — This app features the indoor maps of each hotel as well as a strip map. The hotel maps are very handy for easy of finding places inside hotels. If you want to meet a friend in a hotel, look at the hotel map and pick a location to meet. An example would be the Indigo Lounge in Bally's. The lounge is easy to see on the Bally's map. The app also includes the Monorail map, a road map, and a map of the strip with hotels highlighted.

<u>Heading Compass</u> — This app a very good for ensuring your cardinal directions while navigating around Las Vegas. The digital aspect is very handy.

<u>Gas Buddy</u> — This is an excellent app to help find the cheapest gas in Las Vegas. When you find the cheapest gas, the app also provides directions form your current location. This app will save you money.

Gaia GPS — This app will show your current location on a topographic map that includes boundary lines. This excellent app will help you determine which Las Vegas area jurisdiction you are in.

Sun Surveyor Lite — This app provides an excellent 3D compass of the location of the sun, with time of sunrise, and sunset. The details section provides times for Blue Hour, Sunrise, Golden Hour End, Solar Noon, Evening Golden Hour, and Sunset. This is very good information for photographers, or for anyone who might want to know the sunrise/sunset times for having breakfast or dinner at a rooftop restaurant.

Sol Sun Clock — This app has an alarm clock for sunrise and sunset and shows time for Civil, Nautical, and Astronomical Twilights. This app is excellent for reminding you of these times that are ideal for photography applications. It has an excellent tutorial also.

Speed Tracker — This app is a GPS speed tracker that will ensure that the speedometer on your car is working correctly.

Vegas — This is an excellent app for looking for the lowest prices and comparing prices of hotels, tours, shows, and special deals. From Vegas.com you can book from your mobile phone. This is the app to use to find low priced rooms.

AAA Mobile — This app combines maps, directions and roadside service features with member discount information in one easy-to-use app. AAA Approved and Diamond Rated hotels and restaurants are very handy even for non-members.

PEOPLE FINDER APPS

WishDates — This app is for finding people of like interest around you. It is one of the higher rated of this type of app, with 5 stars and 100% satisfaction.

BreakTheIce — This app can be used for finding people with interests that align with your own. It rates at 4.5 stars with 87% overall satisfaction.

OkCupid — This app for finding people rates at 4.3 stars with 88% overall satisfaction.

ABOUT THE
AUTHOR

Titus Nelson, a writer, professional engineer, and research analyst, has worked on several publications including "Brahe Church: The Count's Treasury," a photo history book about the Brahe Church that is situated on the Island of Visingsö in Southern Sweden. Written in English and Swedish, the book describes the history of the island and the church. This was Silverview Publishing's first publication.

He is currently writing about the 1971 Cannikin underground nuclear test in Alaska, where he and 59 other miners drilled, blasted, and mined out a chamber big enough to fit a 5-story building 6,000 feet under Amchitka Island. The chamber was required for testing the five-megaton Spartan nuclear warhead. The Cannikin test was one of the most controversial nuclear tests ever conducted.

One of his finer achievements was obtaining a Memorandum Of Understanding with three chiefs of the Gitksan tribe of Northern British Columbia for a large eco-tourism project. The signed document was a rare agreement in the history of Canadian-Tribal relations.

Titus Nelson has a degree from Cal Poly San Luis Obispo in California, where he retains the title of Registered Professional Engineer. He is retired from his professional engineering status in the States of Alaska, Colorado, Oregon, Washington, and the Province of British Columbia, Canada. He resides near Las Vegas, Nevada.

You can contact Titus Nelson at info@silverviewpublishing. com.

Additional copies of *Las Vegas Insider's Guide*
are available through your favorite
book dealer or from the publisher:

Silverview Publishing
P.O. Box 778268
Henderson, NV 89077-8268
Phone: 702-533-4363
Fax: 702-534-3989
Website: www.SilverviewPublishing.com
E-mail: info@silverviewpublishing.com

Las Vegas Insider's Guide
ISBN (Print version): 978-0-9840266-1-6 $22.95
(ePUB version): 978-0-9840266-2-3 $11.99
(ePDF version): 978-0-9840266-3-0 $11.99

To contact Titus Nelson:
E-mail: info@silverviewpublishing.com

Distributed To The Trade By:
AtlasBooks Distribution
30 Amberwood Parkway
Ashland, OH 44805
Phone: 800-266-5564, 800-247-6553
Fax: 419-281-6883
E-mail: Order@AtlasBooks.com